BEAUTIFUL

Dr. Thelma Davidson Adair

Rev. Dr. James Hal Cone

Rev. Dr. Otis Moss, Jr.

Sr. Francesca Thompson, OSF

Rev. Dr. Jeremiah A. Wright, Jr.

ARE THEIR FEET...

Romans 10:15 KJV

CELEBRATING MINISTRIES AND GIFTS • VOLUME IV

The Baobab Tree - "The Tree of Life"

ISBN: 0-9765145-1-6

Beautiful Are Their Feet

For whosoever shall call upon the
name of the Lord shall be saved.

How then shall they call on him in
whom they have not believed?
And how shall they believe in him of
whom they have not heard?
And how shall they hear
without a preacher?

And how shall they preach, except they be sent?
As it is written, How beautiful are the feet of
them that preach the gospel of peace, and
bring glad tidings of good things!

Romans 10: 13-15 (KJV)

Rev. Dr. Samuel De Witt Proctor

1921 - 1997

The late Reverend Dr. Samuel DeWitt Proctor was Pastor Emeritus of the Abyssinian Baptist Church of New York City and Professor Emeritus at Rutgers University. Dr. Proctor was president of Virginia Union University, Richmond and North Carolina A&T State University. He held administrative positions with the Peace Corps in Nigeria and Washington, D.C. and the National Council of Churches.

He lectured throughout the world and taught at many institutions, including United Theological Seminary, the Divinity School at Duke University, Kean College and Drew University. Dr. Proctor served on the governing boards of the United Negro College Fund, National Urban League, Colgate-Rochester-Crozer Theological Seminary and the Overseer's Visiting Committee for the Divinity School at Harvard University. He was Pastor-in-Residence for the Institute for Child Advocacy at the Children's Defense Fund/Haley Farm.

An alumnus of Virginia Union and Crozer Theological Seminary, he was awarded honorary doctorate degrees from more than fifty colleges and universities.

Dr. Proctor was a prolific writer and preacher, authoring *We Have This Ministry, How Shall They Hear & Sermons from the Black Pulpit, The Certain Sound of the Trumpet, The Substance of Things Hoped For,* along with many others.

"Those of us who have inherited benefits we did not earn or deserve must help those who inherited deficits they did not earn or deserve [to help them] earn what we take for granted."

"It is one thing to know the "is-ness" of things, and even better to know the "ought-ness," but then comes the "there-fore" of things, where we go and how can we get started."

"One's ministry is incomplete unless one makes a real effort to bring the congregation into a mature awareness of what Christ calls us to do in his name among the least of these."

"Given all the biblical scholarship at hand, and all the analysis of the historical Jesus, one is not likely to be confused about what a society would look like that followed the Jesus paradigm."

"Some pastors have given up on filling the shoes of Amos, Micah, Isaiah or Jeremiah... God bless those pastors who stand tall and who, in love, tell the truth. They are the [watchpersons] in the tower, the sentinels at the gate who can save us from total pollution."

Here is a man who by the very gifts of nature looked like a prince and talked like a poet ... and the word for him was "Be thou faithful."

— Rev. Dr. Samuel DeWitt Proctor

"TREE OF LIFE"

BEAUTIFUL ARE THEIR FEET

It is a gift from God to honor those who serve him. It is a gift from God to honor those whose feet have been blessed and anointed. And it is a gift from the One who guides us to honor the works of those who have set the pace. The five theologians honored today are pacesetters, who represent the best in theological thought and who brilliantly proclaim the Gospel of Jesus Christ. As in the thirty-seventh Psalm, our honorees are blessed men and women whose steps God has ordered and whose works are worthy to be praised. Dr. Thelma Adair, Rev. Dr. James H. Cone, Sister Francesca Thompson, Rev. Dr. Otis Moss, Jr., and Rev. Dr. Jeremiah A. Wright, Jr. are genuine preachers and teachers of liberation and truth for they walk in the way of freedom, mercy and justice. They have opened their souls to God, placed others above themselves and used their ministerial gifts for the Kingdom's good. Their steps are ordered. They have set the pace.
They are gifts from the Lord. And their feet are truly beautiful.

DR. THELMA ADAIR, internationally known church leader and educator, has always been an advocate for peace. Along with her husband, Dr. Adair helped to organize the Mount Morris Presbyterian Church in New York, NY, which was the launching pad for her accomplished career. She has been ecumenical in her approach to ministry, serving as national president of Church Women United, a movement of Christian, Orthodox and Catholic women. She was president of the Black Presbyterian Caucus and, as General Assembly Moderator, Dr. Adair has been a voice for women of faith and an inspiration to those who love the Lord.

She has lectured at Union Theological Seminary, New York City, Columbia University and the University of Ghana. She is Professor Emeritus of Queens College in New York, where she taught for nearly three decades. Dr. Adair always demanded excellence and expected only the best from her students so they could one day possess the land God promised.

Dr. Adair's feet are beautiful because she is a trailblazer who has walked with unquestioned authority throughout western and non-western, rich and poor nations. Her feet are beautiful because whether serving as pastor, mother, grandmother or wife, she has worn a mantle of excellence, leadership and grace.

YOUR STEPS HAVE BEEN ORDERED. YOUR FEET ARE BEAUTIFUL.

REV. DR. JAMES H. CONE, theologian and scholar par excellence, has dared to travel where few have gone. His book, ***Black Theology of Liberation,*** revolutionized and transformed religious studies and, as some have said, was a "searing indictment of white theology and society." His impassioned, skillful writing and public pronouncements leave no question where he stands on setting the captives free.

Dr. Cone's mentor, C. Eric Lincoln, summarized his works by declaring that Cone "almost single handedly re-shaped Western theological thought to make it racially inclusive by demythologizing the conventional myths and shibboleths that kept it a white spiritual and philosophical preserve for centuries." No truer words have been spoken.

As the distinguished Charles A. Briggs Chair of Systematic Theology at Union Theological Seminary in New York and an ordained African Methodist Episcopal minister, Cone's feet are beautiful because he truly talks the talk and walks the walk.

Cone's feet are beautiful because he has not forgotten or rejected his Arkansas roots. His feet are beautiful because he has re-shaped the Christian landscape to include the African American perspective.

YOUR STEPS HAVE BEEN ORDERED. YOUR FEET ARE BEAUTIFUL.

REV. DR. OTIS MOSS, Jr. has traveled a long way from LaGrange, GA. From the hallowed halls of Morehouse College to Atlanta's Interdenominational Theological Center to the Chair of the Morehouse College Board of Trustees to the renowned congregation of Olivet Institutional Baptist Church in Cleveland, Ohio, Dr. Moss has been an undeniable force for change, excellence and the power of the living God.

As one of Dr. Martin Luther King Jr.'s trusted confidants and co-pastor at the historic Ebenezer Baptist Church during the early1960's, Dr. Moss has been in the battlefield for decades fighting for civil rights, human rights and social justice. He is a standard bearer who continues to lead the way. Dr. Moss has received numerous awards and national recognition for the work he has done. And he has walked with political giants and broken bread with kings, but his heart has remained with the people of God.

Dr. Moss' road has not been easy; like Job of old, he has known the heat of the refiner's fire and the anvil of adversity but has come forth like pure gold. His experience has given him a rare and clarified view and has created a certain power for proclamation and a sweetness in the delivery of the Word. His feet are beautiful because he knows the danger of walking the razor's edge where one's feet can be cut. His feet are beautiful because he stayed the course, ran the race and has claimed the victory.

YOUR STEPS HAVE BEEN ORDERED. YOUR FEET ARE BEAUTIFUL.

SISTER FRANCESCA THOMPSON, an Oldenburg Franciscan nun, loves to preach, loves the theatre and loves to teach her students. As a gifted orator and educator, Dr. Thompson has increased understanding and given insight to and appreciation for the rich heritage of the holy Roman Catholic Church and the role and contribution of African ancestored people in it. She believes her call to the sisterhood like other religious vocations was a blessed calling she felt compelled to answer.

Sister Francesca also was a mentor and instructor to the master preachers in the Martin Luther King, Jr., Fellows program in Black Church Studies at the Crozer Divinity School. Reared by her grandmother and her father in Indianapolis, Sister Francesca's gift and love for the written word brought a new dimension to her students' work. She served for a number of years as assistant dean and director of multicultural studies at Fordham University in New York.

Sister Francesca Thompson, in demand as a speaker in churches and on campuses, has enriched the earth wherever her feet have trod.

Her feet are beautiful because she has brought a divine presence of a caring God closer to many who "would have fainted had they not believed to see the goodness of the Lord in the land of the living."

YOUR STEPS HAVE BEEN ORDERED. YOUR FEET ARE BEAUTIFUL.

REV. DR. JEREMIAH A. WRIGHT, JR., is a master theologian, religious scholar, an expert in homiletics and a pastor's pastor. He is a son of the parsonage and steeped in a family heritage rich in education and religion. These foundational strengths shaped Dr. Wright's vast ministry at the Trinity United Church of Christ in Chicago, IL, and throughout the world. Dr. Wright shepherds one of the most politically active and socially conscious churches in the nation, and faithfully ministers to the least, the lost, the locked out and the left behind.

As a third generation family member to matriculate at Virginia Union University and as a graduate of Howard University, University of Chicago Divinity School and United Theological Seminary, Dr. Wright believes in the power of an educated mind. Through Trinity, he supports hundreds of students and seminarians. He has a passion and a love for young people, a dedication to the continent of Africa and a commitment to social justice and peace that is unsurpassed. He, too, is a standard bearer, a theological giant, a faithful man of God who has selflessly led the way for others.

Dr. Wright's feet are beautiful because he has been willing to take giant steps for God's people and has not been limited by the short, mincing tiptoe of indecision. His feet are beautiful because he was one of the founders of the Samuel DeWitt Proctor Conference, Inc. His feet are beautiful because Dr. Wright's good works have leveled mountains and elevated valleys so the glory of the Lord could be revealed.

YOUR STEPS HAVE BEEN ORDERED. YOUR FEET ARE BEAUTIFUL.

The world is a better place because of the faithfulness of these mighty servants of God!

The Rev. Dr. Samuel B. McKinney
Mount Zion Baptist Church, Pastor Emeritus
Seattle, WA

WILLIAM JEFFERSON CLINTON

November 1, 2006

Warm greetings to everyone gathered in New Orleans for the 2007 Samuel DeWitt Proctor Conference. I am delighted to join you in congratulating your distinguished honorees: Reverend Thelma Adair, Reverend James Cone, Reverend Otis Moss, Sister Francesca Thompson, and Reverend Jeremiah Wright.

I have long been convinced that we will be an infinitely better, stronger nation if our efforts are informed by, driven by, and advanced by people of faith. As President, when I worked on issues ranging from teen pregnancy to bridging the digital divide, I always sought the counsel, input, and involvement of our faith community. More and more, we have come to recognize that if we want to effect real change, we must involve our religious leaders.

We have made a lot of progress toward a more equitable society in recent decades and provided fresh opportunities for those who historically have been denied access to the American Dream; but we clearly still have work to do if we are to eradicate the impediments that remain for African Americans struggling to succeed in our society. Your honorees have done much in this endeavor and, just as important, have moved others to do the same. I've had the privilege of worshipping at a service led by Reverend Moss, and I relay all the time the words he said that day, how powerfully he said them, and how inspired he left his congregants to go out and be good citizens and good neighbors.

I'm pleased that you are focusing this year on our continuing commitment to the survivors of Hurricane Katrina. As you know, former President Bush and I established the Bush-Clinton Katrina Fund to assist in the recovery. When I first met with survivors in temporary housing, I was shocked by so much of what I saw, and deeply saddened by what I heard. The outpouring of support in the months following the disaster has helped make a lot of progress toward rebuilding lives and communities, but there still is more to do. I have no doubt that your efforts will help people who have suffered unimaginable loss to rise above the heartbreak and look toward a future full of promise.

Best wishes for a productive conference.

Bill Clinton

BEAUTIFUL ARE THEIR FEET
HONOREE
Dr. Thelma Davidson Adair

*Give her the reward she has earned, and let her works bring
her praise at the city gate.* Proverb 31: 31 (NIV)

BEAUTIFUL ARE THEIR FEET
HONOREE
Dr. Thelma Davidson Adair

"As a mother comforts her child, so I will comfort you."

Isaiah 66:13

In our culture of celebrity worship, there is a tendency to praise individuals for the facades of their achievements rather than for the substance of their work, often work to which they have profoundly dedicated their entire lives. In the case of Thelma C. Davidson Adair, we most often hear of her rise to high office as the "the first woman of color to be honored with the highest elected office of the Presbyterian Church." For sure, her emergence to the post of Moderator of the 188th General Assembly of the Presbyterian Church was, and is still, an outstanding accomplishment worthy of acknowledgement, praise and historical documentation. It symbolized the church's willingness to respect a woman and a person of color as "the first among equals" or "the most senior among a group of church leaders." In these times, such a symbolic gesture is not to be taken lightly.

But looking at the breadth and depth of Thelma C. Davidson Adair's life and work, the bestowal of that honor upon her was far more than a symbolic gesture, far more than a bid to celebrity status. Rather, it was an occasion which affirmed what grassroots people have known about Thelma C. Davidson Adair for decades: specifically, that she is a brilliant visionary leader driven by a lifelong commitment to serve the least of these and thus imminently qualified to guide the Presbyterian Church—or any other church, for that matter—in the fulfillment of its God-given mission.

The daughter, niece and sister of Baptist clergymen, Thelma C. Davidson Adair was born to a legacy of high achievement and a faith-based commitment to helping others. As intimate witnesses of her devout praxis, her children and grandchildren attest to her emphasis on spiritual, physical and intellectual development in lessons she taught them and others. They tell us that, with these lessons, she sought to make them ready and able to take on the complex issues of morality, health, faith and education that characterize our local, national and global communities today. And they insist that model—of hard work equating to excellence, intellectual ability defining opportunity, and spiritual and physical health translating to wholeness -- was evident at all times. Her grandchildren maintain that these were, in fact, the hallmarks of her effective and principled leadership, which inspired a generation of men and women throughout the world to be great and to work for positive change.

One of six siblings, Thelma Davidson was born on August 30, 1920, in Iron Station, North Carolina. Her mother, the former Frances Wilson, was a mortician and teacher, and her father, Rev. Robert J. Davidson, was a minister, school principal and farmer. From the very start, the young Thelma showed the traits of precocity and compassion. She learned to read by age three, two years before she went to elementary school; and, phenomenally, at age ten she entered high school.

In four years, at age fourteen, she graduated from high school and enrolled as a freshman at Barber-Scotia College, a Presbyterian institution in Concord, North Carolina. Recalling her academic progression and its inherent call to stewardship, Dr. Adair explains, "It was expected that we study the year around, including summer and winter. We were always taking courses and teaching the other children in the neighborhood."

Continuing the pattern of those foundational years, Thelma Adair went on to major in history and science at Bennett College and graduated magnum cum laude with a Bachelors degree—at age eighteen. She then began her teaching career in small schools and, as fate would have it, met and eventually married Arthur Eugene Adair. They settled in Chester, South Carolina, and began planning their future. Four years later, in 1942, given his call to ministry and her commitment to teaching, the Adairs decided to pursue graduate studies in New York City. With him headed to Union Theological Seminary and her to Columbia University's Teachers College, they sold their 1936 Chevrolet for $500 to finance the move to New York, a turning point in their lives. "We had just built a little house in Chester, South Carolina," Dr. Adair explains, "We shut the door, planning to be back in June." But once in New York—more specifically, once in Harlem—they never returned to Chester.

Immersed in their studies and finding themselves amid the lingering richness of Harlem's cultural renaissance, the intellectual stimulation of it all proved far more captivating than expected. And their contribution to that milieu came into focus. Indeed, as Arthur Eugene Adair began actualizing plans to found the Mount Morris Ascension Presbyterian Church of New York in 1944, Thelma Adair worked by his side. Taking the people of Harlem to heart and with insight into their needs, she helped establish Mount Morris New Life, a children's day care center, as a key mission of the church.

Over the years the center grew and was eventually renamed The Arthur Eugene and Thelma Adair Community Life Center Inc. Head Start, serving hundreds of children and their families in six different locations throughout Harlem. Emerging as Director of the Arthur Eugene and Thelma Adair Head Start Program upon the completion of her doctorate, Thelma Adair instituted programs that actualized her belief that education is the cornerstone in the development of people. Sharing insights derived from professional involvement with children and families, her numerous published works on early childhood education have become authoritative guides for early childhood educators throughout the United States.

Paralleling her work with children, Dr. Adair emerged as a theologian and taught religious education at Colgate-Rochester Seminary, Princeton Theological Seminary, New York Theological Seminary and was named Distinguished Professor of Religious Education at her late husband's alma mater, Union Theological Seminary in New York City. Her presence was sought at religious and secular conferences around the world. To highlight some, she served as coordinator of the Church Wide Christian Education Conference in Liberia, West Africa; the United Nations Mid-Decade Forum in Copenhagen, Denmark; the Jerusalem Women's Seminar in the Middle East; and as education coordinator for Peace Corps programs throughout the Caribbean and in the United States. She was also leader of the Asian Women's College Seminars on Continuing Education in Pakistan, India, Korea, Singapore and Japan; the Church Women United Peace Causeway in Taiwan, Japan, Australia and New Zealand; and the Asian Women's Conference in Australia, Fiji and Singapore.

Of course, throughout her life Dr. Adair has been very active in the Presbyterian Church—in New York, across America and abroad. She is the Ruling Elder of Mount Morris Ascension Presbyterian Church, a lifetime appointment. And she has served the Presbyterian Church's Evangelism & Church Development Ministry Unit, its Council on Religion and Race, its Committee on Christian Education, as Chairperson of its World Service Department, Secretary of its National Missions initiative and a member of its Executive Committee. She also served as the Presbyterian Church, U.S.A.'s Official Delegate to the Millennium Celebration of the Russian Orthodox Church in the USSR and as Moderator of the Church's General Assembly Mission Council. But, ultimately, it was Thelma Adair's election as Moderator of the 188th General Assembly of the United Presbyterian Church in the U.S.A. which occasioned the discovery and celebration of her as "a first."

Time will tell how Dr. Thelma C. Davidson Adair is remembered. Given the enduring politics of race and gender - yes, even in the church - the world may choose to recall her as another in a series of "firsts." But if our historical memory is to be accurate, we will recall the scope and dedication of her work and, thus, take our mnemonic cue from her husband, the late Reverend Dr. Arthur Eugene Adair. Throughout their years together, he witnessed the constancy and depth of her motherly love for their children, the children of others and people in general. And in his final sermon, a moving tribute to Thelma Adair, he chose a text that poignantly summarizes her operative belief, her praxis: "As a mother comforts her child, so I will comfort you." Isaiah 66:13

"Go on. You Can Do It."

Born in Iron Station, NC - August 30, 1920

BIOGRAPHY HIGHLIGHTS
Bachelor of Arts, Bennett College, Greensboro, NC; Master of Science and Doctor of Education, Columbia Teacher's College, New York, NY

First African American woman to become moderator of the Presbyterian General Assembly; Several honorary degrees; NAACP Distinguished Award for Outstanding Service; Sojourner Truth Award for National Business and Professional Women; Community Service Society of New York City

MINISTRY FOOTPRINTS:
Founder and Director of The Mount Morris Day Care Center
Arthur Eugene and Thelma Adair Community Life Center

SOWING THE GOOD SEED

Dr. Thelma Davidson Adair

As Stated Clerk of the General Assembly of the Presbyterian Church-U.S.A., it gives me great pleasure to join many others in paying tribute to Dr. Thelma Davidson Adair. It is especially appropriate that the Samuel DeWitt Proctor Conference, Inc has chosen to honor Ms. Adair in the year that the church is celebrating triple anniversaries of women's ordination – 100 years for deacons, 75 years for elders and 50 years for ministers.

Thelma Davidson Adair, a Presbyterian Elder and retired university professor, was one of the first women elders at Mount Morris Presbyterian Church in New York City. She was the second woman – and the first woman of color – to serve as moderator of the General Assembly of the United Presbyterian Church in the United States of America, a predecessor denomination of the current Presbyterian Church-U.S.A.

As moderator, Thelma traveled around the United States and abroad speaking out on many issues, particularly around education, justice, human rights and the civil rights movement. No one can equal her oratorical skills, which she continues to use within the Presbyterian Church and in ecumenical circles, to champion causes such as economic justice, violence against women, AIDS, full participation of women in the church, and racism. Her concern for social justice is rooted in her faith in Jesus Christ.

Thelma Davidson Adair is a real gift from God to the Presbyterian Church (U.S.A.) and to the church ecumenical, and I thank God for her.

Clifton Kirkpatrick
Stated Clerk of the General Assembly
Presbyterian Church (U.S.A.)

A WOMAN FOR ALL SEASONS

Dr. Thelma Davidson Adair

Thelma C. Davidson Adair has been a woman for all seasons. She has been an educator, a writer, a scholar, an advocate for justice, a witness for peace, a public speaker, a spokesperson for the poor, and a committed servant of humankind.

Among Presbyterians she is known foremost as a church leader. She is an ordained elder in the Mount Morris Ascension Presbyterian Church (U.S.A.) in New York City, NY. This church was founded and organized in the early 1940's by her late husband, the Reverend Arthur Eugene Adair. She has served at Presbytery, Synod, and General Assembly levels of the Presbyterian Church (U.S.A.).

Thelma became the first woman of color elected Moderator of the Presbyterian Church's 188th General Assembly in 1976. She has served as national president of Black Presbyterians United (BPU) and as president of the Northeast Region Caucus of BPU.

She was recognized for her service to Johnson C. Smith Theological Seminary with both the title of Trustee Emeritus and the honorary degree of Doctor of Humane Letters. She has been articulate and passionate in promoting the ministry of the seminary over the years. As a result of her partnership with other trustees, the seminary is poised to implement a capital campaign to build its first building on the campus of Interdenominational Theological Center (Atlanta) and to raise additional funds to provide increased scholarship aid to seminarians.

In the Old and New Testaments there are so many passages of what blessings look like: "of rivers running where once only deserts were, of lions laying down with lambs, of fields of wheat swaying and singing in the breeze, of every person having her own shade and fig tree…"

It is so wonderful when our lives are enriched and empowered by one of God's special servants who tries to embody the teachings of Scripture and gives us a paradigm of how we should seek to bless those we come in contact with along life's journey of faith.

Along with the community of faith, Johnson C. Smith Theological Seminary salutes Dr. Thelma C. Davidson Adair, who has blessed our lives in loving and caring ways.

David L. Wallace, Sr.
Dean, Johnson C. Smith Theological Seminary

BEAUTIFUL ARE THEIR FEET
HONOREE
Rev. Dr. James H. Cone

The people were amazed at his teaching, because he taught them as one who had authority, not as the teachers of the law.
Mark 1:22   (NIV)

BEAUTIFUL ARE THEIR FEET
HONOREE
Rev. Dr. James H. Cone

"…I knew in the depths of my being that European and American approaches to theology did not deal with the questions arising out of my experience…"

James Hal Cone was once referred to as the "upstart young Black theologian" who caused something of a theological "earthquake" with the publication of his book *A Black Theology of Liberation* in 1970. A searing indictment of white theology's long-standing appropriation of religious thought and practice to the service of racism and oppression, Cone's book positioned him at the forefront of ongoing discourse and advocacy of what some call the Black Theology revolution. His essential belief is: "Any message that is not related to the liberation of the poor in a society is not Christ's message. Any theology that is indifferent to the theme of liberation is not Christian theology."

An unknown junior professor at Michigan's Adrian College at the time of his emergence as a voice for change in the church in America and around the world, James Cone grew up in the small town of Bearden, Arkansas. And it was there that he began to understand the contradictions between black and mainstream theological perspectives on the practice of faith as lived experience. In *God of the Oppressed*, another work of his, Cone reveals "At Macedonia African Methodist Episcopal Church, I encountered the presence of the divine Spirit, and my soul was moved and filled with an aspiration for freedom. Through prayer,

song and sermon, God made frequent visits to the black community in Bearden and reassured the people of God's concern for their well-being and the divine will to bring them safely home…that 'otherworldly' reality beyond the reach of the dreadful limitations of this world. Every Sunday the black brothers and sisters of Macedonia experienced a foretaste of their 'home in glory' when God's Spirit visited their worship, and they responded with thankfulness and humility, singing joyfully:…" Cone continues, "but unfortunately the black church experience was not my only experience in Bearden, Arkansas. The presence of 800 whites made me realize, at an early age, that black existence cannot, indeed, must not, be taken for granted. White people did everything within their power to define black reality…they tried to make us believe that God created black people to be white people's servants. We blacks, therefore, were expected to enjoy plowing their fields, cleaning their homes, mowing their lawns, and working in their sawmills. And when we showed signs of displeasure with our so-called elected and inferior status, they called us 'uppity niggers' and quickly attempted to put us in our 'place.' Cone adds, "…their affirmation of faith in Jesus Christ was a source of puzzlement to me, because they excluded blacks not only socially but also from their church services… Because I have lived the Bearden experience, I cannot separate it from my theological perspective. I am a black theologian! I therefore must approach the subject of theology in the light of the black church and what that means in a society dominated by white people…"

Currently the Charles A Briggs Distinguished Professor of Systematic Theology at the Union Theological Seminary in New York City, James Cone earned his Bachelor of Divinity degree from Garrett Theological Seminary in 1961, and his Masters degree and Ph.D. from Northwestern University in 1963 and 1965, respectively. In his current post, Dr. Cone teaches various courses, among them *Foundations in Christian Theology, Black Theology, Theology From The Underside of History, Reinhold Neibuhr, Martin Luther King Jr.* and *Malcolm* X and seminars in Christology, Ecclesiology and the topic *God, Suffering & The Human Being.*

An ordained minister in the African Methodist Episcopal Church, James Cone is a prodigious author and speaker. Along with his lectures at more than 700 colleges, universities, divinity schools and community organizations throughout the world, he has written numerous scholarly articles. Books he has authored include *God of the Oppressed, Risks of Faith: The Emergence of Black Theology Liberation, The Spirituals & The Blues: An Interpretation, Martin & Malcolm & America: A Dream or a Nightmare, A Black Theology of Liberation, For My People: Black Theology and The Black Church, Speaking The Truth: Ecumenism, Liberation and Black Theology, James H. Cone & Black Liberation Theology Black Theology* and *Ideology: Deideological Dimensions in the Theology of James H. Cone.* In 1992, *Ebony Magazine* awarded him the "American Black Achievement Award" in religion. Two years later, the Association of Theological Schools gave him their Theological Scholarship & Research Award.

But fully cognizant that his is a call to speak truth for the empowerment of others, rather than a call to pursue the personal celebrity of honors and awards, over the decades of his emergence Dr. Cone has repeatedly revisited and expanded his theology of liberation to focus on more than racism. Accordingly, Cone tells us "Although my view of white theology is generally the same today as it was in 1970, there are several significant shifts in my theological perspective…" He explains that his focus now also embraces the call for human liberation from "…sexism, the exploitation of the Third World, classism and inordinate dependence upon the neo-orthodox theology of European theologians."

Dr. Cone's wide renowned and many speaking appearances around the world might suggest wide acceptance of his theory and views, especially since his theology of liberation embraces all oppressed people, i.e. women, homosexuals, Africans as well as African Americans, Hispanics, Asians and the poor everywhere. But Gayraud Wilmore reminds us of the deep resistance Cone still faces. In an essay titled "A Revolution Unfulfilled but not Invalidated," Wilmore observes, " It [Cone's theology of liberation] opened up a brand new school of theological method and social action that most American Christians, black as well as white, were totally unprepared for and have not yet thoroughly understood, much less appropriated."

But despite such a lack of preparedness, lack of thorough understanding and the apparent lack of a widespread will to act among theologians and the church in general, Dr. Cone sees a different and positive change dynamic afoot in the world. He observes, "Though evil seems more prevalent and powerful today than yesterday, people are still resisting. Resistance creates hope. Just as Jesus' resurrection was born out of his apparent defeat on the cross, so too the poor are born anew out of their resistance to suffering. The irruption of the poor is happening in African, European, Hispanic, Indian, and Asian communities in the U.S. and throughout the world. Their resurrection is the sign that God is at work in the world, raising the dead to life. We must join the resistance by making solidarity with those who struggle for life in the face of death."

Thus, Dr. Cone remains steadfast in his advocacy of liberation theology in the operative beliefs and lived experience of daily life. He tells us, "I believe more strongly than ever that black theology's reason for being is defined by the liberation struggle of the poor. It must not, therefore, seek merely to be an academic discipline, reflecting on intellectual matters interesting to university and seminary professors and their graduate students. Rather, black theology must be the prophetic voice of the church, proclaiming throughout the world what Amos said nearly 3,000 years ago: 'Let justice roll down like waters and righteousness as a mighty stream.' Without this voice the church ceases to be the church, and theology ceases to be Christian."

The Spirit of the Lord Is Upon Him

Born in Bearden, Arkansas - August 5, 1938

BIOGRAPHY HIGHLIGHTS:
Bachelor of Arts, Philander Smith College, Little Rock, Arkansas; Bachelor of Divinity, Garrett Theological Seminary, Evanston, Illinois; Master of Arts and Doctor of Philosophy, Northwestern University, Evanston, Illinois

Charles Augustus Briggs Distinguished Professor of Systematic Theology, Union Theological Seminary; recipient of numerous honorary degrees

PUBLICATIONS:
Author of numerous articles and 11 books, including *Black Theology of Liberation* (1970) and *God of the Oppressed* (1975)

MINISTRY FOOTPRINTS:
Father of Black Theology; Black Theology Project

A GIFT OF EPOCHAL SIGNIFICANCE!

Rev. Dr. James H. Cone

JAMES HAL CONE

Dear Brothers and Sisters:

African Americans have always been generic theologians, but black theological thinkers, with or without the Ph.D, have been scarce: John W.E. Bowen, Jr. of the Methodist Church; Henry M. Turner and Benjamin Tucker Tanner of the AMEs; Alexander Walters, AMEZ; Edward Wilmot Blyden, Presbyterian; Rufus L. Perry, Benjamin E. Mays, George Kelsey, J. Deotis Roberts, and Martin Luther King, Jr., Baptists; Marcus M. Garvey of the U.N.I.A.; George Alexander McGuire of the African Orthodox Church; and Jaramogi Abebe Agyeman of the Black Christian Nationalist Church. A few more could be mentioned. None of these, however, gave us a black systematic theology. That distinction belongs to James Hal Cone. In three pathfinding works, *Black Theology and Black Power* (1969), *A Black Theology of Liberation* (1970), and his opus magnus, *God of the Oppressed* (1975), Cone laid down the distinguishing earmarks of what can justly be called a black theology of liberation, the first genuine counterpoint to Euro-American Christianity to be written and taught by a black professional theologian since the 16th century Reformation.

Cone has produced more black Ph.Ds in systematic theology at Union in New York than anyone past or present. Most of us who teach and write "God-talk" that explicates the religious meaning of the African American experience take our positions either in apposition or studied opposition to James Hal Cone.

Agyeman may have discovered the Black Messiah, but Cone revealed him as the Second Person of the Triune God, the Liberator--Jesus of the New Testament. An achievement of epochal significance!

Gayraud S. Wilmore

THE TIDAL WAVE

Rev. Dr. James H. Cone

Dr. James H. Cone is one of the most significant theologians of our time. He earned the highest degree in his field and then transformed that academic discipline into a field of study that bears the indelible marks of his critique and constructive engagement. There was a time when Christian theology could go about its work as if the black experience of slavery and segregation were irrelevant to the Gospel of Jesus Christ. That was B.J.C.—before Jim Cone. Through his unrelenting attack against racism and the idolatrous presumptions of white theology, what had generally been ignored gained a central and defining place in systematic theology. Jim Cone made the case that blackness and Christianity were not strangers. They were companions in the struggle—upstaged by amazing grace.

Beginning with the publication of Black Theology and Black Power in 1969 and A Black Theology of Liberation in 1970, the tidal wave of black theology changed the landscape of theological education and altered the course of sociopolitical thought in colleges and universities in the United States and around the world.

Jim Cone was called to the Christian ministry as a teenager. No one could have known at that time the scope, focus, intensity, persistence, and eventual impact his ministry would have. It unfolded with certain passionate priorities. I cannot read the Great Commandment without hearing Jim Cone's special challenge to the church. The commandment says, "Thou shalt love the Lord thy God with all thy heart, all thy mind, and all thy strength, and thy neighbor as thyself." First, Jim Cone accepted the task of reminding us that we must love the Lord with our minds. For him, uncritical devotion shortchanges any faith claim. He had seen too much fervor without the accompaniment of disciplined thought.

A second emphasis had to do with the call to love the self. Having grown up in a culture where black folks had been forced to see themselves through the eyes of oppressors, liberation from self-loathing had to be a key component of saving grace. Stokeley Carmichael may have shouted "Black power" with raised fist, but Cone gave the theological foundation for the transformed consciousness of black affirmation and black power.

A third emphasis had to do with loving the neighbor. Cone taught us that Christianity was not authentic if it missed this explicit call of the Great Commandment. He sought to invalidate the faith claims of people who filled churches but insisted on maintaining walls of separation on account of race, religion, gender, or class. Such a clear critique of mainline religion was more than many could take. For Cone to sustain that kind of judgment required extraordinary courage and deeply rooted conviction, but he never backed down. He endured the scorn and weathered the storm of criticism and contempt, but kept on bearing witness to the Gospel's case for liberation.

After writing 11 books, teaching nearly half a century, lecturing all over the world, and preaching the gospel of liberation, Dr. Cone shows no sign of weariness in the struggle. His mind is constantly at work to unearth new approaches for promoting justice and compassion. One of his mentors, the late C. Eric Lincoln, lived long enough to see his young colleague come into the full flowering of his magnificent ministry. He said, "James Hal Cone has almost single-handedly reshaped Western theological thought to make it racially inclusive by demythologizing the conventional myths and shibboleths that kept it a white spiritual and philosophical preserve for centuries."

I am honored to have known Jim Cone and have worked as his colleague and friend for over 30 years. I have experienced the constancy of his commitment in word and deed to the gospel of liberation. He is indeed a living legend. We are honored to be companions with him in the continuing work of liberation.

Rev. Dr. James Forbes

BEAUTIFUL ARE THEIR FEET
HONOREE
Rev. Dr. Otis Moss Jr.

For Moses said, "The Lord your God will raise up for you a prophet like me from among your own people; you must listen to everything he tells you."
Acts 3:22 (NIV)

BEAUTIFUL ARE THEIR FEET
HONOREE
Rev. Dr. Otis Moss Jr.

*The answer will be determined by what we do now,
how we serve God in the present*

Reflecting on *A Knock at Midnight*, the anthology of sermons by Martin Luther King, Jr., the Rev. Dr. Otis Moss explained "We must draw strength from the deep reservoir of Dr. King's wisdom. It is midnight, but dawn is coming. There is a 'knock at midnight' in every age, every decade. We can and must respond." Though Moss clearly meant it in tribute to Dr. King, that statement prophetically referenced himself too. After all, like Dr. King, Moss has been involved in the struggle for social justice and civil and human rights his entire life.

He tells us, "My decision to enter the ministry was a gift or calling from God. I was greatly influenced by my hometown church community and spiritual leaders. My mentor was Dr. Benjamin E. Mays, President of Morehouse College in Atlanta, Georgia. He provided encouragement and inspiration. And an abiding friendship and association with Dr. Martin Luther King, Jr. provided great inspiration and an excellent model for leadership." Having been a staff member of Reverend Dr. Martin Luther King, Jr., Dr. Moss also served as co-pastor to Dr. Martin Luther King, Sr. at Atlanta's historic Ebenezer Baptist Church. And now, some four decades later, Moss still serves as a national board member and trustee for the Martin Luther King, Jr. Center for Non-Violent Social Change.

While the inspiration of Drs. Mays and King in-

fluenced the direction of his calling, surely Dr. Moss was also influenced by the lived experience with racism and injustice. This aspect of his emergence is indicated when he tells of the humiliation his father, Otis Moss, Sr., experienced when he attempted to vote in Jim Crow Georgia. As the story goes, Otis Moss, Sr., a poor sharecropper who worked all his life to provide for his family, suffered indignities and humiliations that generations of blacks before him had long endured. For the first time, in his 50s, Otis Moss Sr. went to cast his vote. On Election Day, he rose before dawn, dressed in his best suit, which was normally reserved for funerals and weddings, and prepared to walk to the polls to vote against a racist Georgia governor, in favor of a moderate.

He walked for six miles to reach the first polling station and, when he got there, he was told he was in the wrong place and sent to another location. He walked another five or six miles and met with the same denial, and was sent to a third voting place. When he arrived at the third location, they told him, "Boy, you are a little late – the polls just closed." Thus, after walking all day, covering more than 18 miles, Moss Sr. returned home, exhausted and depleted, denied of his right to vote. In the days, months and few years that followed, the elder Moss told this story to anyone who would listen, both to purge the hurt and to rally others. Undaunted, he lived in great anticipation of his next chance to cast his vote; but he died before the next election and never got the chance to vote.

As a witness to his father's ordeal, and no doubt the racist ordeals suffered by others and himself, Otis Moss, Jr. saw the pursuit of social justice as a focal theme of his life and ministry. Now, decades later, Moss' record shows a steadfast commitment to his calling. And as a preacher, theologian and activist, he has used his platform as a pastor - at Provident Baptist Church in Atlanta, Mt. Zion Baptist Church in Cincinnati and now Olivet Institutional Baptist Church in Cleveland – to be a voice of conscience in matters of social justice, civil rights, and human rights.

Dr. Moss tells us, "The role of the church is salvation, liberation and reconciliation. The three cannot be separated. Salvation through faith in Jesus Christ is fundamental. But salvation without liberation is not salvation at all. It is a feel-good religion that does not impact a person's economic, social, political and civic standing. You cannot preach the gospel without getting involved in social policy. The church has the ability to be the conscience of a community."

Of course, as is indicated by highlights of his extensive career, Moss' spheres of influence suggest that he uses the term "community" to apply globally and nationally, as well as locally. Recognized around the world, his work has taken him to China and Korea, where he was feted as a special guest at Taegu University, and Japan, where he was featured as guest minister for the Tokyo Baptist Church. And he has been a member of clergy missions to the Far East and the Middle East. He was also the special guest of former President Bill Clinton at the Peace Treaty signing between Israel and Jordan and, in that same year, he led a special mission to South Africa. He is also a member of the Oxford University Roundtable.

As a nationally recognized leader, he is credited with numerous other honors and achievements. He served as a consultant to former U.S. President Jimmy Carter and as featured guest lecturer for the joint U.S. Army and Navy Martin Luther King programs.

A Life Member of the NAACP and Alpha Phi Alpha fraternity, he is also the recipient of the Bethune Cookman College Human Relations Award, the American Jewish Committee Leadership Award, the Ohio Governors Civil Rights Award and a member of the Harvard Review Committee. He has served as a guest presenter for the Lyman Beecher Lecture series at Yale University. Currently Chairman of the Board of Trustees at Morehouse College, he also serves as an Adjunct Professor at United Theological Seminary in Dayton, Ohio.

But, his global and national recognition notwithstanding, it is his work at the local level, with the grassroots, that attests to the essence of the life and ministry of Rev. Dr. Otis Moss. Indeed, as pastor of Olivet Institutional Baptist Church, in Cleveland, since 1975, he has profoundly touched the lives of thousands of people, both directly and exponentially. Here, he has emphasized political self-empowerment within a faith-based context, telling his followers that "…we often narrowly view politics as something that should be left to other people, that we as religious people should not be 'tainted' by it. But we get our Social Security cards and Medicare cards through the political process. We are all affected by public policy issues and governmental institutions. Dr. King recognized that we could participate in public policy issues and be true to the ministry of Jesus Christ. The two are not divorced but inextricably tied together."

Rev. Dr. Otis Moss Jr.

Acting on the strength of that conviction, Dr. Moss has galvanized Olivet's advocacy and attainment of such essentials as the following: a job opportunities referral service; a state-of-the-art medical center to provide inner-city residents with more accessible, quality health care; an education fund to provide community residents with financial assistance to attend college; an emergency food pantry and clothing program; and innovative counseling programs to help ex-offenders and substance abusers restore themselves to productive, creative and Christ-centered lives. These and other initiatives implemented through Olivet's outreach ministries, under Dr. Moss' leadership, have positioned the church on the cutting edge of service and relevance in ways that model praxis for other communities throughout the country.

Of course, Otis Moss is a highly learned man. He holds a bachelor's degree from Morehouse College, a master of divinity degree from Morehouse School of Religion/Interdenominational Theological Seminary, an earned doctorate of ministry from Union Theological Seminary and numerous honorary degrees for other institutions. He is also a family man, married to the former Edwina Hudson Smith, with three children: Kevin, Daphne (deceased) and Otis Moss III. These aspects of his life, along with his work, have endowed him with a profound sense of continuity and a focus on intergenerational accountability that speaks to us all.

Thus, when he asks the members of Olivet Institutional Baptist Church to contemplate and envision the future, he is not speaking simply to them but to all of us in every community of faith. We must all take heed when he says *"The larger question is what kind of congregation and community will we have one hundred years from now? The answer to the above question will be determined by what we do now, and how we serve God in the present."*

**God Gives Us Vision.
It's Up to Us to Embrace It.**

Born in LaGrange, Georgia - February 26, 1935

BIOGRAPHY HIGHLIGHTS:
Bachelor of Arts, Morehouse College, Atlanta, Georgia; Master of Divinity, Morehouse School of Religion/Interdenominational Theological Center, Atlanta, Georgia; Doctor of Ministry, United Theological Seminary, Dayton, Ohio; National Board Member and Trustee for the Martin Luther King, Jr. Center

Recipient of numerous awards, honors and honorary degrees

MINISTRY FOOTPRINTS:
Otis Moss, Jr. University Hospitals Medical Center; Otis Moss, Jr. Residential Suites - Morehouse College

JIMMY CARTER

February 5, 2007

To the Reverend Dr. Otis Moss

Rosalynn joins me in congratulating you on being honored at The Samuel DeWitt Proctor Conference. It is fitting that your example of excellence is being recognized in this way. You can take great pride in the exemplary service you have provided your community throughout your long and distinguished career.

I would like to share a few lines I wrote about you in my book <u>Living Faith</u>:

> *The most unforgettable funeral I've ever attended, maybe with exception of my own family members, was the service for Mrs. Martin Luther King, Sr., mother of our nation's greatest civil rights leader. Her husband, Daddy King, and the whole family were close friends of ours. I and a number of other speakers made brief comments, but there was one truly memorable presentation. Rev. Otis Moss from Cleveland, Ohio, preached a brief but remarkable sermon about "the little dash in between." He said there would be a marker on Mrs. King's grave, with her name and a couple of dates – when she was born and when she died – and a little dash in between. He said he didn't want to talk about when she was born, or when she died, but about the little dash. He described Mrs. King's great life and then shifted his attention to the audience. He said that everybody has what might be considered just a tiny dash but that to us, with God, it is everything.*

We join the attendees of this important event in sending you our warm best wishes for continued happiness and fulfillment.

Sincerely,

Jimmy Carter

Honor Thy Father

Rev. Dr. Otis Moss Jr.

"I recognized the gift but I did not open it until years later." While this statement has a peculiar sound, it echoes the sentiment of most who love their fathers. We recognize the gift but we do not open what has been given to us until time allows our hearts to hold the precious narrative of love fathers breathe into the lives of little boys searching for direction. My recognition day of your power and precious love was witnessed in 1982 as I sat with the deacons as a "junior deacon" under the leadership of Hoover Thomas. My task was to run the back-up tape recorder for the Audio Ministry. I was always excited about "having a hand" in making your word last beyond the present age. It was an ordinary Sunday. Sister Barbara Collier, as always, directed the choir with Pentecostal power and the Deacons attempted to teach us, the youth, common meter hymns for devotion. During your sermon the tape ran out, nothing out of the ordinary, but as I attempted to move next to the pulpit and turn the tape over, I glanced up at you and sweat poured from your brow and your voice penetrated the church with authority. In that moment, God gave a little boy a glimpse into a man's soul. I watched as the hand of God held you and a glow encased your body. You were my father, but at that moment I witnessed my father touched by God's hand. It was this brief moment where your entire ministry came together in a celestial nexus.

> ## *God gave a little boy a glimpse into a man's soul.*

The love you demonstrated daily for Mom – you love Mom with such a powerful quietness. You tell her "I Love You" and you show this in private and in public; the dignity you demonstrated during Daphne and Kevin Jr.'s deaths; the fatherly direction, fun and correction you have shown to me and Kevin. Many men are honored for what they do for the community and the church, but I honor you because you never allowed the words Preacher and Father to become an oxymoron in our household. You speak justice but pillow fight with your children. You walked with Dr. King, Septima Clark, Adam Clayton Powell and Howard Thurman but still found time to walk with your family. The true measure of a man is not what he does in public, but that his private life is in sync with his public walk. Your walk has been in step with God! Now as I look at my children, I pray I can be half the father you have been in my life and half the husband you have been to Mom.

I recognized the gift given to me as a boy and now, as a man, I am able to handle the gifts of dignity, honor, faith, respect, love, passion, forgiveness, humor and gentleness.

Love, Otis

As For Me and My House...

Rev. Dr. Otis Moss Jr.

...We Will Serve The Lord

BEAUTIFUL ARE THEIR FEET
HONOREE

Sr. Francesca Thompson, OSF

She opens her mouth with wisdom, and the teaching of
kindness is on her tongue.
Proverb 31:26 (RSV)

BEAUTIFUL ARE THEIR FEET
HONOREE
Sr. Francesca Thompson, OSF

"…to represent the underrepresented, to teach, to learn, to serve."

In 2002 Sister Francesca Thompson retired from nearly a quarter century at New York's Fordham University, where she served multiple roles as assistant dean and director of multicultural programs, and associate professor of African and African American studies. The occasion also marked her half century as an African American nun in the Franciscan Order. But the general public probably knows Sister Francesca Thompson as "that Black nun on the board of the Tony Awards," the prestigious Broadway honors given to legitimate theater artists by the Antoinette Perry Foundation.

For at least two reasons, it is fitting to relate Sister Francesca to theater. First, her association reminds us that theater, as one of the oldest and most important art forms of cultures worldwide, derives from religious rituals. Noting this, Sister Francesca once dared a bit of ecclesiastical humor when she quipped "Jesus must have been part actor, musing over his theatrical backdrops—the sermon preached against a mountain setting, a wedding as the scene of his first miracle, walking on water, and his triumphant entry into Jerusalem on Palm Sunday." And second, it is said that Sister Francesca (whose birth name is Edeve) was born with theater in her blood. Here reference is made to her

parents, Edward Thompson and Evelyn Preer, both gifted actors and members of *The Lafayette Players*, the legendary Harlem-based troupe that proved to be one of the longest running stock companies in American theater history.

Her parents' background in theater had a profound effect on Sister Thompson's work as an educator and scholar. From 1966 to 1982, during her early years as a Franciscan nun, she taught theater arts and English at Marian College in Indianapolis, and during that period also completed her doctorate in speech and drama at the University of Michigan. While at the University of Michigan, she also served as an acting coach for actresses Gilda Radner, who rose to fame on NBC's *Saturday Night Live*, and Christine Lahti, who went on to become a major film star, and several other budding actors.

But the central focus of her time at the University of Michigan was the development of her doctoral dissertation on the history of *The Lafayette Players*. This was an inspired accomplishment that she approached with doubt. Indeed, when it was first suggested that she should research her parents' theatrical troupe, Sister Francesca had doubts about the availability of written material on the troupe and doubts about her ability to track down original players who were still alive to authenticate oral history accounts of the troupe. But, opting for a kind of action research to resolve key questions and overcome her doubts, Sister Francesca decided to send out the kind of "begging letters" nuns use to secure donations of everything from money to hard goods to in-kind services for their churches. However, Sister Francesca's begging letters were sent to editors of Black newspapers, beseeching them to run ads and editorials about her search for information on *The Lafayette Players*. Well, no doubt because she promised the editors "Black power in Heaven," they responded to the plea and helped her establish contact with three members of the Lafayette Players, including the founder.

Sister Francesca's dissertation is a moving and brilliant tribute to The Lafayette Players as a symbol of persistence in the cultural war of that time. As an important historical document, it not only positions her as the keeper and protector of her family history, but also as the scholar who has kept the legacy of The Lafayette Players in the forefront and, by extension, instilled pride in many Black artists who have struggled to be recognized. Too, because it demonstrated the depth and breadth of her overall knowledge of theater as an art form and discipline, Sister Francesa's doctorate helped her become chairperson of Marian College's drama and speech department. In that capacity, she taught about life, morality and ethical values in works by American and international playwrights, poets and novelists, white and black. For example,

her study of Eugene O'Neill's many works delves into his tempestuous relationship with organized religion and Catholicism in particular.

Far from the cloistered existence we sometimes imagine about nuns, Sister Francesca's life is the stuff of an informed worldview. In a real sense, she was called to a higher understanding of life at seven months of age when her mother died of pneumonia at 35 years of age. Then, raised by her father and grandmother, both of whom modeled heightened social and political consciousness, Sister Francesca grew up in a home frequented by such "conscious" people as actor/singer/activist Paul Robeson, actress Ruby Dee, musician Eubie Blake and others – all friends of her father. And, because her grandmother was a powerful Democratic ward captain, their home was often visited by city politicians, clergymen, judges and even Indiana's gubernatorial candidates. Thus, in that setting, Sister Francesca – as Edeve the child – imbibed awareness of the struggle. She often tells how her father cautioned her to the reality of racism with words she has never forgotten: "Some people might think you're inferior," he said to her, "but it will be only a manifestation of their ignorance."

Sister Francesca admits to having heard horror stories about racism and harassment in religious orders and the church overall. But, surprisingly, such ordeals have not been her personal experience. Rather, she clarifies that her challenge was her own lack of humility. Recalling her entry into the St. Francis of Oldenburg some 50 years ago, she is reminded of her young self as being "…so vain and arrogant, it was nearly impossible for my novice mistress to smack some humility into me." She adds, "I honestly thought that the sisters of my community sat up all night clapping their hands when they heard I was joining them." But along the way, as the lessons of faith brought her calling into sharper focus, she learned humility. One indication of this is her favorite aphorism— "If you want to make God laugh, tell him your plans."

Of course, through the lived experience of her faith, she has developed her sense of praxis to which others readily give witness. Thus, it is said that whether in the posh executive offices occupied by the Tony Awards Board members or in an overcrowded inner-city classroom, the mission of Sister Francesca Thompson has always been the same: "to protect the legacy, to represent the underrepresented, to teach, to learn, to serve."

You Catch More Flies with A Spoonful of Honey than A Barrel of Vinegar

Born in Los Angeles, California - April 29, 1932

BIOGRAPHY HIGHLIGHTS:
Bachelor of Arts, Marian College, Indianapolis, Indiana; Master of Education, Xavier University, Cincinnati, Ohio; Doctor of Philosophy, University of Michigan

Franciscan Sister of Oldenburg; Executive Board Member for Martin Luther King, Jr. Fellows; National Black Sisters Conference

MINISTRY FOOTPRINTS:
Tony Awards Committee; Use of arts to promote racial understanding

A Troubadour for Jesus

Sr. Francesca Thompson, OSF

The Lafayette Players

Anyone who knows Sister Francesca Thompson, OSF, a member of the Oldenburg Franciscans, knows her as a woman who lives life to the full! (John 10:10) Named Edeve at birth, she was renamed Evelyn to honor her deceased mother Evelyn Preer Thompson who, with her father, Edward Thompson, was an early member of the original Lafayette Players. Her grandmother's wisdom and self-sacrificial love for others and her parents' commitment to the theatre were transmitted to and transformed by Sister Francesca. She combined her family's charisma with that of St. Francis of Assisi, a rich man who renounced his wealth to serve and celebrate the presence of God in everyone and everything. Francesca, like Francis, seeks God in the depth of her heart and mind, knowing full well the necessity of taking seriously the injunction of Psalm 36: "Be still and know that I am God!" In that stillness, Sister Francesca communes with Jesus.

Sister Francesca, like Jesus, is a woman who lives her life totally for others. Called to be a troubadour for Jesus, she prepared herself by completing a bachelor degree in English, a master's degree in Communication Arts and a Ph.D. in Theatre and Speech. The knowledge garnered from her life experiences and formal education, has been used to enrich others whom she served as an educator, drama teacher, director, and administrator, to proclaim and embody God's universal love and justice. She is nationally known and held in high esteem in diverse circles of influence: the Christian ecumenical world of Catholic and Protestants, in the academic world of university professors and administrators and numerous education organizations; in the world of justice-seeking social activist organizations, and in the national and international world of the theatre.

In the Catholic Community, particularly the Black Catholic Community, Sister Francesca is revered and sought after because of her ability to use gentle humorous persuasive language and drama to awaken her audience's consciousness and hearts. She has spent a lifetime helping us to come to know ourselves and others by helping us explore the meaning of life, love and God through dramatic performance. To know Sister Francesca is to taste the joy of being invited to be with a person who lives in the presence and beauty of a loving, creative and humorous God who reveals himself through others.

Sr. Dr. Jamie T. Phelps, O.P. (Ph.D.), Director
& Katherine Drexel Professor of Systematic Theology
Institute for Black Catholic Studies
Xavier University of Louisiana,
New Orleans, Louisiana

BEAUTIFUL ARE THEIR FEET
HONOREE

Rev. Dr. Jeremiah A. Wright, Jr.

And whether they listen or fail to listen — for they are a rebellious house —
they will know that a prophet has been among them.
Ezekiel 2:5 (NIV)

BEAUTIFUL ARE THEIR FEET
HONOREE
Rev. Dr. Jeremiah A. Wright, Jr.

*"Jesus did not come to make heaven a better place.
He came to make heaven on earth."*

Jeremiah Wright is often hailed as one of the greatest living preachers. He gives a contemporary African-American and Afrocentric flavor to the traditional Black "shout" and he blends a Pentecostal flavor with social concerns in his pulpit discourse. It is also said that one of his sermons is a four course meal: spiritual, biblical, cultural and prophetic. So, clearly, Wright's preaching deserves accolades, which he views as proof of his obeisance to the central importance of the sermonic tradition. Yet it must be noted that accolades and celebrity for preaching are not his goal or objective, because Jeremiah Wright is more than a preacher.

Indeed, in an overarching sense, the substance of Jeremiah Wright's work and achievements position him as a symbol, an example of faith in action, the embodiment of praxis informed by devotion and a theology of liberation. During the Power Preaching Conference at the Lutheran Theological Seminary of Philadelphia, Wright explained that "…Jesus did not come here to make Heaven a better place. He came to make Heaven on Earth." Thus, with Jesus as his example, Wright revealed that his goal, his objective, is the betterment and fulfillment of people, the realization of

"heaven on earth," if you will, borne of truth, compassion and justice.

A native of Philadelphia, Wright is the son of Rev. Jeremiah Wright, Sr. and Dr. Mary Henderson Wright, both of whom, as defining influences, raised him to seek a meaningful life of stewardship, characterized by balancing the intellectual with the spiritual. Given this philosophical upbringing, and in preparation for the work of such a life, the young Wright earned a Masters degree from the University of Chicago Divinity School and a Doctor of Ministry degree from the United Theological Seminary in Dayton, Ohio, where he studied under Samuel DeWitt Proctor.

Beyond his academic credentials, earned and honorary, Jeremiah Wright's ongoing intellectual and spiritual development is reflected in his discourse and collaborations with other clergy, grassroots people, community activists and his work as theology professor at such institutions as the Chicago Theological Seminary, North Park Theological Seminary, the Seminary Consortium for Urban Pastoral Education and the Lutheran Theological Seminary of Philadelphia. He has taught courses in the Black religious experience, the history and meaning of the Black Church, structure and process in the Black community, general homiletics, Afrocentric preaching and pastoring and, of course, liberation theology in the Black Church.

But those achievements notwithstanding, the depth of philosophical upbringing and development over the years are perhaps best reflected in Wright's leadership of Trinity United Church of Christ, in Chicago, for over three decades. During that time, the church has grown from 87 members to a congregation of nearly 10,000, making it a so called "mega-church." Though Wright would never take sole credit for such phenomenal growth, nevertheless, Trinity's growth is the result of his faith-based vision and praxis, and his role in helping the church define itself to itself, in relation to God, to its community, to the mainstream church and the society at large.

Under his leadership, Trinity has lived by the motto ***"Unashamedly Black and Unapologetically Christian"*** and has set out to make activism within and on behalf of the African American community a key aspect of the church's mission. An outspoken community leader, Wright has been vocal in making once-taboo issues, such as AIDS, a priority within the African American church leadership and service. His outspokenness, which helps to purge the dysfunction of individuals and communities, along with his commitment to political activism and the African American sermonic tradition, have placed Trinity United Church of Christ at the center of a movement for the betterment and fulfillment of people, the realization of "heaven on earth."

Along with this, Wright has shepherded

Trinity's embrace of a value system of precepts and covenants to shape and enrich the practice of faith. This value system prioritizes commitments to God, the Black community, the Black family, to education, the work ethic, self-discipline, self-respect, stewardship and the disavowal of beliefs and practices that encourage ascendancy, that "crabs in the barrel" phenomenon that has historically undermined unity among African Americans.

Inherent to this value system, Wright has led the church's cultivation of a multi-faceted vision of positive possibilities centered around faith-based concepts of adoration, salvation, reconciliation, and commitments to Africa, biblical education, cultural education, the liberation of all people, restoration and working towards economic parity.

The genius of Wright's leadership is that these foundational values and visions are actualized in Trinity's outreach ministries, the result being that he and his congregation "live and act faith," not just "preach faith."

At present, there are more than 70 active ministries. Too numerous to list in their entirety, the ministries' respective foci address areas that range from academic, legal and crisis counseling to media technology, prison outreach, HIV/AIDS, music, reading enhancement, sign language and computer learning. A massive and sustained programming effort, the ministries signal Wright's attentiveness to the lives and needs of people in Black communities.

Finally, of all that can be said of Rev. Dr. Jeremiah Wright, one of the most beautiful and moving is the Mission Statement of Trinity United Church of Christ. Though it was probably developed by a committee, it is resonant with his imprimatur as a man who balances the intellectual with the spiritual for the betterment and fulfillment of others:

Trinity United Church of Christ has been called by God to be a congregation that is not ashamed of the gospel of Jesus Christ and that does not apologize for its African roots. ...we are called to be the agents of liberation not only for the oppressed but for all of God's family. We, as a church family, acknowledge that we are building on this affirmation of "who we are" and "whose we are," call men, women, boys and girls to the liberating love of Jesus Christ... We are called out to be a "chosen people" that pays no attention to socioeconomic or educational backgrounds...

I Will Bless The Lord At All Times!

Born in Philadelphia, Pennsylvania - September 22, 1941

BIOGRAPHY HIGHLIGHTS:
Bachelor of Arts, Virginia Union University, Richmond, Virginia; Master of Arts, Howard University, Washington, DC; Master of Arts, University of Chicago Divinity School, Chicago, Illinois; Doctor of Ministry, United Theological Seminary, Dayton, Ohio

US Marine Corps, 1961-1963

Recipient of numerous awards, honors and honorary degrees; Board of Trustees, Virginia Union University

PUBLICATIONS:
Author of four books and numerous articles

MINISTRY FOOTPRINTS:
Global Ministry

PRIEST AND PROPHET

Rev. Dr. Jeremiah A. Wright, Jr.

An Expression to Dr. Jeremiah A. Wright, Jr.

Many of the biblical epistles conclude with expressions of thanks to the Creator and gratitude to those persons whose presence and partnership blessed the lives and ministry of the writers. I could follow the model and easily give thanks to all the individuals we honor this year and especially my teacher and mentor, Dr. James Cone. I am privileged, however, to express appreciation and give tribute in a particular way to Dr. Jeremiah A. Wright Jr., my friend, my brother, and fellow servant for well over thirty years.

Jeremiah's unique and immense gifts of mind, person, and spirit give witness to the awesome Creator who gives life and deposits in the life of all distinct goodness and Godness. Throughout his ministry, he has wedded the priestly and prophetic dimensions of ministry in a creative, courageous and consistent manner. With discerning "street" wisdom, genuine human sensitivity, deep intellect and flowing spirit, he has informed and transformed the character of individuals, ministry, communities and our world. With sanctified imagination, poetic, magical, and powerful pronouncement, convergent scholarship and authentic being, Jeremiah has helped us see the hidden, discover deeper meaning, celebrate history and life, pursue truth and justice, and claim the promise of the "not yet."

As an evolved soul, his gifts and capacities have never led him to shrink himself into petty, self-promoting agendas. He has never lost common sense and common touch and his anointing has never been threatened by genuine presence with all people. With wit, wisdom, energy and integrity, he has been and continues to be a remarkable, faithful servant of God.

Jeremiah, I thank God and I thank you. Be not weary in well doing…

Rev. Dr. John W. Kinney

UNITED STATES SENATE
WASHINGTON, DC 20510

BARACK OBAMA
ILLINOIS

February 5, 2007

Dear Friends:

I would like to extend warm congratulations and best wishes to my pastor, Rev. Dr. Jeremiah A. Wright, Jr., who has been presented with the Samuel DeWitt Proctor Conference's highest honor. It is truly a pleasure to join you in appreciating Rev. Wright -- my mentor, my pastor, and my friend.

When I think of Rev. Wright, I recall the book of Hebrews. As you know, an unknown author wrote this text in response to the fears and doubts of the new Christians of that time. Hebrews was intended to calm their hearts, and impart wisdom that would strengthen their faith during trying times -- the return of Jesus had not happened when expected, and the long-term endurance of the Christian faith was unclear. After thirteen chapters, the author concludes with words of guidance to the early Christians, as they traversed their daily struggles:

"Remember your leaders, who spoke the word of God to you. Consider the outcome of their way of life, and imitate their faith."

Indeed, when those of us who have been touched by Rev. Wright over the years find ourselves in need of guidance, we know where to turn. As Hebrews wisely instructs, we remember our leader; we consider how he lives his life; and we imitate his persistent and audacious faith.

I constantly remember Rev. Wright as the shepherd who guided me to my commitment to Christ one Sunday morning at Trinity United Church of Christ. I often consider, as I work in the Senate, how he lives his life – a life of service to Trinity, Chicago, and the nation; his activism on behalf of causes that few would champion; and his dogged commitment to the first principles of love for God and fellow man. And in my personal walk, I seek daily to imitate his faith.

To all those attending the Proctor Conference, I regret that I could not be present during this momentous occasion. However, I ask that you formally add my voice to the sincere chorus of thousands who honor Rev. Dr. Jeremiah A. Wright. There is no leader more worthy of our remembrance, consideration, and imitation, as we work to fulfill both our personal purposes, and the goals that we all share.

Yours sincerely,

Barack Obama
United States Senator

A Wife Like No Other!

Rev. Dr. Jeremiah A. Wright, Jr.

My name is John B. Williams. Jeremiah and I were bunk-mates in the United States Marine Corps, stationed at Camp LeJuene, North Carolina, back in the early 1960s. We were in the 2nd Division band and our duties were to play morning colors (the raising of the Flag,) and evening colors (the lowering of the Flag). Jerry played the clarinet and I played the drums. We thought that playing in the band would keep us from such thing as guard duty, forced marches, war games, having to go out in the North Carolina boondocks to biv'ouac (camp out in the woods without the luxury of a tent) to simulate actual combat conditions. We thought that the BAND would be our escape from all that, but the band was part of the Headquarters Battalion, whose job it was to protect the Command Post. However, we did get the chance to go to New York City to play for the opening of the World's Fair and march down 5th Avenue as a part of the Armed Forces Day Parade.

Then we got shipped off to Guantanamo Bay, Cuba, during the "Bay of Pigs" standoff. On the flip side we had to march around the Base playing the "Death March" when John Kennedy was assassinated. Through it all Jeremiah Wright and I formed a friendship and a bond that we will share for the rest of our lives. I forgot to mention that when two Marines share the same bunk beds, they (we) refer to one another as "WIFE". So we would take turns running errands and making trips to the gee-donk (vending machines). We never used our names; it was always, "Hey wife, would you do this or that for me?"

> **Through it all Jeremiah Wright and I formed a friendship and a bond that we will share for the rest of our lives.**

Our time in the Marines was made more interesting due to being Black and stationed in the South in the early 60s. But, through it all, Jeremiah was always positive, intelligent, and he always had a knack for making the best out of a bad situation. I was happy, but not too surprised, when Jeremiah told me, years after we were both separated from military service, that he was pastoring a church in Chicago. I sort of felt that this was his calling. So every time I'm in Chicago, I make it a point to attend Sunday service at Trinity United Church of Christ and spend some time with him and his beautiful family.

I am proud of Rev. Wright, and I am happy to have been his USMC "WIFE," and blessed beyond measure to be his **FRIEND**.

John B. Williams

Rev. Dr. Otis Moss Jr.

Samuel DeWitt Proctor Conference, Inc.
4533 South Lake Park Avenue
Chicago, Illinois 60653

It is a privilege for me to join you in honoring the Reverend Dr. Otis Moss, Jr., as the Samuel DeWitt Proctor Conference celebrates him and his contributions to our lives and times.

Brother Otis Moss has meant so much to me in my work since I met him with Dr. Martin Luther King, Jr., over forty years ago. He had been jailed in the south during a sit-in demonstration. We developed a spiritual kinship, a bonding around a shared vision of the Beloved Community, the vision so dear to Dr. King. Even as a young man, Otis stood out as such a profound preacher. Dr. King once was discussing with some friends who were the ten most profound preachers that they knew. As the others named several great preachers, Dr. King jumped in and said "before you get to ten, don't leave out Otis Moss!" It was remarkable to gain such respect at such an early age. And of course, his renown has continued to grow.

Wherever he has served – in Georgia, in Cincinnati, in Cleveland – he has been a powerful advocate and activist, and a sound theological interpreter for social justice. His theology has driven him to attend to the needs of everyone, even "the least of these" – all our brothers and sisters. He served on the board of PUSH, and helped guide us through times of challenge and change. He has always been ready to respond when I have called upon him to help or advise. I owe him much. He is indeed a marvelous servant of our Lord because he intends to be of service to all.

Sincerely,

Jesse Jackson

Reverend Jesse L. Jackson, Sr.
Founder and President
Rainbow PUSH Coalition Inc.

JLJ:gfm

THE WORD IS NEAR YOU, IN YOUR MOUTH AND IN YOUR HEART…ROMANS 10.8 (NASB)

Rev. Dr. Otis Moss Jr.

My dear friend and pastor, the Rev. Dr. Otis Moss, Jr., has beautiful feet, indeed, and I have been blessed to walk alongside him for some forty years as we journey toward justice for children, the poor, and all who endure injustice in our rich nation.

Those feet carried him through the storied halls of Morehouse College, Morehouse School of Religion/ITC, and finally across the stage of the United Theological Seminary to receive his Doctor of Ministry as he answered the call to ministry. Whether stepping into the sanctuary of Atlanta's Ebenezer Baptist Church with Dr. Martin Luther King, Sr., into the White House as an advisor to President Jimmy Carter, or into the pulpit of Olivet Institutional Baptist Church where he now serves, Dr. Moss has proclaimed with power and passion the word God placed in his mouth and heart.

Dr. Moss' beautiful feet brought the good news of peace as he marched alongside Dr. Martin Luther King, Jr. and others in the Movement. When I was a senior at Spelman College and he was still a student at ITC, Otis was our pastor in the sit-in movement in Atlanta, praying for us as we prepared to march across town despite KKK threats, making us ready to be arrested and making us ready to die nonviolently if necessary.

Dr. Moss continues to walk a path of nonviolent social and political change as a religious leader and community activist, and stands with those who are poor, lack health care, and suffer injustice. Through the Otis Moss Jr. University Hospitals Medical Center in Cleveland's Fairfax neighborhood, Dr. Moss has demonstrated what it means to truly serve as Christ's hands and feet here on earth to some of our nation's 46 million people without health care coverage. He is listed as "one of the 30 people who has defined Cleveland over the past 30 years," but I would add that he is one of the people who has defined being a Christian over those same years.

As a preacher, Dr. Moss has stepped into pulpits across the nation and preached the powerful and prophetic word that is in his heart. True, with a voice so rich and deep we would happily listen to him read the phone book, but it is the Gospel of our Lord and Savior Jesus Christ that is ever on his lips. Dr. Moss' incomparable preaching has rightly earned him a place on Ebony's list of our nation's "15 Greatest Black Preachers," but I would respectfully amend that to simply declare that he is one of our nation's 15 Greatest Preachers, period. One of the hallmarks of Dr. Moss' preaching is that it transcends boundaries, defies limitations, and speaks powerfully to all with ears to hear.

For the past ten years, Dr. Moss' feet have walked the holy ground of Children's Defense Fund's Alex Haley Farm in Clinton, Tennessee each July. There he serves as the Pastor-in-Residence of the Samuel DeWitt Proctor Institute for Child Advocacy Ministry. He was the only person I could imagine filling the mighty big shoes left behind by Dr. Proctor, and he has not only done so but left his own indelible mark on our minds and hearts. (His son, Otis III, evidently inherited not only Otis Jr's good looks but also his beautiful feet, as he serves alongside his father as co-Pastor-in-Residence at Haley.) On behalf of the thousands of faithful child advocates he has sustained and renewed, comforted and challenged, lifted up and sent forth to continue their work for justice, I offer him my deepest gratitude.

Dr. Otis Moss, Jr., is a good and faithful companion on this journey toward justice whose proclamation of the gospel sustains us and illumines the way ahead. I look forward to continuing to walk and march and stand for children and the poor with him until every child and family in our nation experiences the good news of peace and justice.

Marian Wright Edelman
Children's Defense Fund

PHENOMENAL WOMAN

Sr. Francesca Thompson, OSF

The Maya Angelou poem, *Phenomenal Woman,* comes to our minds when we think of our cousin, Sister Francesca Thompson, for she is a phenomenal woman. The poem speaks of self-pride and pride inspired by others and our cousin is a proud woman in the best sense of the word and certainly inspires pride in others.

Sister Francesca, or Evelyn as she is known to us, is the keeper and protector of our family history. She has kept the legacy of our family alive and this makes us proud. She has celebrated and kept the legacy of the Lafayette Players in the forefront and, by extension, instilled pride in many black artists who have struggled to be recognized.

She is a teacher and the students who have been lucky enough to have studied with her are filled with her pride. Her teaching goes far beyond the classroom and every time she takes the pulpit or the podium, we are inspired to think a little harder about the world around us.

So whether in the lofty spaces occupied by the members of the Tony Board or in an overcrowded inner-city classroom, her mission has always been the same: to protect the legacy, to represent the underrepresented, to teach, to learn, to serve.

Now you understand
Just why my head's not bowed
I don't shout or jump about
Or have to talk real loud
When you see me passing
It ought to make you proud.

Maya Angelou

Proud we are and proud you should be. We love you much and always.
Congratulations!

From your cousins,
Vicki Meyers, George Knox, John Knox, Addie Knox Jones, Craig Knox,
and our families.

Sr. Francesca Thompson, OSF

EVELYN PREER

MAKING DISCIPLES OF ALL NATIONS

Rev. Dr. James H. Cone

Professor James H. Cone has been the most enduring dialogue partner, inspiration and, dare one say, "hero" for the greater part of the last decade or so of my life. It was in the autumn/fall of 1992 that I was introduced to an excerpt from his first book, **Black Theology and Black Power**, published in 1969. I was struggling at the time with my Christian faith. Having been nurtured with a white majority ecclesial setting, I had witnessed, at first hand, the extent to which the Christian faith had so easily colluded with the notion and the practice of white supremacy and racism in my country. I wondered how and in what way any conscious Black person could remain within the Christian fold. Dr. Cone's writings not only offered me a radical conception of the nature and intent of God's liberating work in Jesus Christ, it also inspired me to want to become a religious scholar.

...inspiring a whole generation of fledging Black British theologians

I would credit Professor Cone with not only inspiring me to go back to the university to enroll in a master's course, which subsequently led to a Ph.D., but also with inspiring a whole generation of fledging Black British theologians. When Professor Cone came to Birmingham in 1997 on a lecture tour, I had the honor of sitting next to him in the restaurant after one of his speaking engagements. For over an hour, poor Professor Cone sat in almost statuesque silence as my peers and I struggled to engage him in conversation. The man was an icon and we were in awe.

Thankfully, there have been several subsequent occasions for conversation and dialogue, but I remain in awe. Professor James H. Cone is the reason I am writing this piece and have the temerity to dare call myself a Black theologian.

Thank you and God bless.

Dr. Anthony G. Reddie
Research Fellow and Consultant
Black Theological Studies
British Methodist Church
The Queen's Foundation
Editor, Black Theology, an international journal

OUR PASTOR, REV. DR. JEREMIAH A. WRIGHT, JR.

Rev. Dr. Jeremiah A. Wright, Jr.

You are a Black Man who is a preacher, pastor, and person without peer!

As your Pastoral Staff, we count it a privilege to honor you. Pastor Wright, you have inaugurated a paradigm shift in the Black Church that is tantamount to the paradigm shift in theology brought on by Dr. James Cone: shifting from worshipping as Europeans to worshipping as our African selves; shifting from learning the story of others, to learning and affirming our own story as African people; shifting from focusing only on a vacant salvation to focusing on a vital salvation informed by and with education and scholarship; shifting from tolerating untrained clergy to pushing for trained and prepared clergy; shifting from a focus of being too heavenly-minded to concentrating on being some earthly good. Your intricate integration of Black Culture and Bold Christendom in your preaching and teaching has set a model of ministry for all who are serious about the cultural, physical, mental and spiritual liberation of Black people everywhere.

For 35 years, you have walked in the mold of Jesus as a servant leader. For 35 years, you have refused to be bought, rented, or sold by any political plotters. For 35 years, you have had a non-negotiable commitment to the liberation of Africans in Diaspora, and Africans on the Continent. For 35 years, you have been a jewel in our fight for justice, a soldier on the Sovereign's battlefield, a powerful proclaimer of God's peace and power, a penetrating professor of God's purpose and of the story of our people. For 35 years, you have been consistent in preaching Christ, calling a cold and callous world to consciousness. Moreover, you are not so insecure as to hoard all of your gifts to yourself. You are a selfless servant, not afraid to release whatever you have in order to enrich the lives of others. As God has blessed you, you have committed yourself to be a blessing to others. In many fields of human endeavor, it is often said that legends, in spite of their own personal accomplishments, were able to make the people around them better and strive for excellence. In addition to the impact on your immediate surroundings, you have changed the landscape of ministry to God's people.

We celebrate Black History year round, not just in the shortest month of the year. And in this month we celebrate walking Black History! We are giving you your flowers now, while you may smell the beauty of their fragrance. You are a great Black Man who is Unashamedly Black and Unapologetically Christian! A Black Man who is not afraid to be who God has called him to be. A Black Man who serves as a model of what it means to be faithful. A Black Man who serves as a model of what Black people can be when they are faithful to God and to God's people.

The Pastoral Staff of Trinity United Church of Christ

For your faithfulness as a brother and for your love as a Pastor, I give God thanks! You are a blessing to the body of Christ!

Rev. Barbara Heard

Congratulations to you, my pastor and my partner in life, love and ministry! To God be the glory for the things He has done for all of us through you!

Rev. Ramah E. Wright

For being there when the Lord called me, thank you! For being there and listening lovingly when my life was in Liminal space, thank you! For teaching me that we should never change who we are because of where we are, thank you! For honoring the Souls of Black Folk by letting the spirits that dwell in deep woods speak through you, thank you! For all these and more, I thank God that he made you a Pastor!

Rev. John Edward Jackson, Sr.

Dear Rev,
As a personal tribute, I offer one short word of thanks that means more than an entire page could relay. I thank you for being faithful to Marcelle's request as intercessor, and all that it entails, both past and present. Thank You!

Rev. Reginald W. Williams, Jr.

Congratulations Pastor Wright!
How blessed I am to have you as my pastor. May God continue to strengthen, comfort and keep you. May God bless you with every good and perfect gift. And may the Lord's richest blessings surround you today and always. Your sister in Christ,

Rev. Regina E.M. Reed

Pastor Wright,
Congratulations! I give thanks to God for the numerous ways that you have blessed my life! Thank you for your love, encouragement and compassion! Thank you for being my father away from home and for your friendship! Thank you for being a prophetic presence and proclamation! Thank you for enriching my life and ministry! It has been an honor and a privilege to be your partner in ministry! Please know that I love you and thank God for you!

Rev. Stacey L. Edwards

Dear Pastor Wright:
In 1994, while in seminary at Howard University School of Divinity, you told me to keep the Spirit of God and I would be okay. You were right! The Spirit of God continues to be my blue print as I journey ahead. Thank you and God bless you!

Rev. Ann Patton

The night is beautiful,
So the faces of my people...

Beautiful, also, is the sun.
Beautiful, also, are the souls of my people.

-Langston Hughes

Beautiful are the feet of the prophets who proclaim the Gospel to God's people. Beautiful is the word which best describes the ministry of Pastor Jeremiah Wright. He loves God with an unshakeable beauty. He communicates the word with poetic beauty that catapults the listener into the heart of the Gospel. We honor this man of beauty, boldness and poetic brilliance. We honor our Pastor, community prophet, theologian, mentor and friend. We honor the beauty in him that touches others who sail in his wake. May the beauty we witness in his life and ministry find a resting place upon our souls.

May the Spirit of the Lord fall fresh upon your life.
Rev. Otis Moss, III

Dear Pastor Wright,
In Luke 15, when the young man came to himself, he remembered to go to his father and ask for forgiveness. Like that father, you waited, welcomed, and did not condemn, as I struggled to answer the call to ministry on my life.
Thank you!
Rev. Michael D. Jacobs

Pastor Wright,
Your encouraging call and message to me as I stood to preach my father's homegoing blessed me beyond words. I thank God for you in my life as a father (Papi) and teacher (Mwalimu). Your example of Christian manhood inspires me every day of my life!
Rev. Cedric L. McCay

For your legacy of faith and a lifetime of faithfulness, nothing seems more adequate than to say, "Thank you" and "I love you!"

Rev. Michael Sykes

A MODERN DAY PROPHET

Rev. Dr. Jeremiah A. Wright, Jr.

When most of us first heard the Rev. Dr. Jeremiah A. Wright, Jr., we were moved.

He was no ordinary, run-of-the mill preacher. He was a preacher with fire in his bones, the likes of which we had never heard before. There was no pretense in his preaching, but plenty of intensity. There was brilliance and evidence of extensive education, research and thought. There was humor and pathos; there was compassion and anger; there was urgency and pleading.

We were hearing a modern-day prophet, and we knew it.

We clamored to listen to him, to study with him and to gain his advice and insight. He mentored us all. He loved us all. He cared for us all.

But, bigger than that, we realized that he cared, he cried, he ached for God's people of African descent. There was no shame in his preaching, no apologizing for who he was and for what he stood. He didn't care that some would criticize him for lifting up the issue of race in his sermons, the issue of oppression of God's people of color and the hypocrisy of Christians who didn't recognize or talk about that fact. He made us all think about the African origins of Christianity and not be ashamed to talk about it and to teach it. He taught us that we, as African Americans, were no mistake, but that we had been hoodwinked by Western society to think that way. We were "unashamedly black and unapologetically Christian," and we'd better know it!

He had an uncanny way of being able to reach all of his listeners – from the very young to grandparents. He would sing the latest R&B songs or quote from a recent rap as easily as he would break into a Brook Benton or Gladys Knight favorite – but not for show. He did it to keep our attention and to remind us all that the Word of God was not and is not a "used to be" phenomenon, but something that we must know and use now.

We've watched him pastor. He "pastors" all over the world. Never had we seen someone reach out to so many people, so consistently. His heart is that of a pastor, and his flock is all over the world. We've watched him embrace his sheep and been amazed at how the sheep have responded to God through the voice of this great modern-day prophet.

He heard, we think, the prophet Isaiah, when that prophet, hearing a voice say, "Cry!" and he answered, "what shall I cry?" Jeremiah A. Wright challenged us to hear the voice of God's people crying, specifically God's people of African descent. He brutally cut into the conceptions and misconceptions that we as sun-kissed children had about ourselves, things about our skin color, lip size and even the size of our hips! He reminded us that all those things were keeping us from hearing the voice of God and the voices of God's children crying because of oppression and racism.

But while he lifted up the plight of us as African Americans, he didn't for a moment allow us to sit and feel sorry for ourselves. No, he wanted us to know who we were and Whose we were and he challenged us, through his preaching, to make a difference, to go out into the world and to serve with a new appreciation of who we were as African Americans.

Thus, the conference. He wanted to bring together people from the church, the academy, the non-profit sector and the corporations, to make a difference. He wanted us to understand how spirit-filled African Americans, in every sector of life, can work together and bring about the Kingdom of God for all. The vision was clear: the conference was to get the old and the young, the educated and the not-so educated, the rich and the poor, all of God's people together for a common good: to be trained and inspired to speak truth to power. This vision was like a fire, burning in his bones, like that of his namesake, the prophet Jeremiah. He was inspired by his mentor, the late Rev. Dr. Samuel DeWitt Proctor, who also had a fire in his bones for social justice. The mentor taught his student and the student, aptly taught, passed the lessons on.

We are honored to serve on the Board of the Samuel DeWitt Proctor Conference. We are honored to honor this great man of God. We are honored that you are here to help us honor him.

Surely, God has smiled on this modern day prophet.

Board of Trustees
Samuel DeWitt Proctor Conference, Inc.

THE QUINTESSENTIAL BLACK THEOLOGIAN AS ACADEMICIAN

Rev. Dr. James H. Cone

What a joy it is for me to write a few words in honor of James H. Cone. I met Jim several years ago in the fall semester of my final year in the Master of Divinity program at the Howard University School of Divinity. He was a visiting professor who had been invited to Howard by Dean Lawrence N. Jones to teach an introductory course in Black theology. I was excited about taking the course from this young scholar who was already a legend in his own time. He had first come to my attention when, as a college student, I was exposed to his explosive first book: *Black Theology and Black Power*. Like a hand grenade thrown into the middle of an unsuspecting crowd, this provocative masterpiece shook up the academy, rattled the church, and shattered all previously held notions about the incompatibility of the Christian faith and the Black revolution.

To sit at the feet of "the father of Black theology," as he has come to be known, was to take a front row seat before the ever unfolding drama of living history. Not only did Jim understand the historical roots of Black theology, but he was the personification of its contemporary systemization. His articulation of its development, therefore, was not simply that of an attentive eyewitness or an astute third party, but rather that of a key player, a prime mover, a driving force, a guiding light who was intimately and passionately immersed in the subject matter he taught. Thus, we seminarians considered ourselves extremely fortunate and rarely privileged to enjoy a private, weekly audience with this refreshingly radical trailblazer of Black theological thought and reflection. Little did I know at the beginning of that class that at its conclusion, he would invite me to come to New York City to study with him at the Union Theological Seminary in pursuit of my Doctor of Philosophy degree in systematic theology. His invitation was an offer I could not refuse.

As one who already held a deep respect and admiration for the man and his work, I grew to appreciate Jim even more at Union as I witnessed firsthand his dedication, his quest for excellence, and his unwavering commitment to identify, train, and develop a cadre of young women and men who would continue, enrich, and, indeed, perpetuate the groundbreaking work of Black theology. He was not content with the personal acclaim he earned as a prolific author whose voluminous works are known and quoted throughout the world, nor was he satisfied with the distinction of being one of only a few African American theologians with a Ph.D. who taught at a prominent theological institution. He was on a mission to produce more Black and ethnic Ph.D.'s in theology. This selfless habit of leveraging his own success in order to open doors through which others might also succeed has phenomenally increased the ranks of liberation theologians on the faculties of seminaries and theological schools throughout the world. It has also guaranteed the establishment of Black and womanist theologies as legitimate disciplines for academic study and inquiry. Finally, it has assured that the Church—both the black church and the church universal—will always be challenged by a critical voice that both reveals its strengths and exposes its weaknesses. Thank you, Jim, for allowing me to be your colleague, your brother, and your friend.

Dr. Dennis W. Wiley, Ph.D.

Rev. Dr. James H. Cone

*I*t is an honor to pay tribute to Dr. James Cone who is fondly spoken of as the father of Black Theology. More than any one theologian, Dr. Cone has changed the course of theological thinking to embrace the radical ethics of Jesus. In doing this, Dr. Cone brought theology out of the speculative and theoretical dialogue of abstract discourse to a down to earth encounter with racism, neocolonialism, nationalism, and the many forms of evil that dehumanize, degrade, and destroy human life. Dr. Cone has courageously challenged the racism in the white church and bravely taken the black church to task for her lack of a prophetic voice and for her hesitation to bravely confront the anti intellectualism and worship as entertainment theme which many so called Black clergy and lay persons embrace.

...the probing and penetrating words of Dr. Cone...pierce our comfort zone and remind us that we are accountable to God for our ministry malpractice and our anemic brand of Christianity.

No living Black Christian educator has trained as many Black theologically trained scholars as Dr. Cone. Many of us in the pastorate continue to revere, relish and reflect on the probing and penetrating words of Dr. Cone, which pierce our comfort zone and remind us that we are accountable to God for our ministry malpractice and our anemic brand of Christianity.

The many established and upcoming womanist writers and the scholarly men in the academy who fuel our faith and motivate us to think critically and to humbly practice our faith are the offspring of the rich teaching legacy of Dr. James Cone. I am personally indebted to him for being my pilot for prophetic ministry as well as a true and treasured friend.

Dr. J. Alfred Smith, Sr.
Senior Pastor
Allen Temple Baptist Church
Oakland, California

FROM HARLEM TO AFRICA

Dr. Thelma Davidson Adair

Thelma Davidson Adair could never be equated with the Laodiceans (Rev 3: 14-16) who were "luke-warm" in their service and love for Christ. Instead, her expression of her faith bubbles over. She leads with fervor, inspiring and challenging others to do the same.

As remarkable as it was to see her elected as the first Black female moderator of the United Presbyterian Church in 1976, even more remarkable have been her contributions to the church, the community and the world. So, it was not just the honor of being the first Black female lay moderator of the General Assembly but the position provided the opportunity for her to expand her witness and for the church to hear the gospel according to Thelma.

Growing up in an atmosphere where both her parents were teachers and her father also a minister, she learned early the importance of education. She began college at Barber Scotia College at age 13. She completed liberal arts studies at Bennett College, and after marriage to a Presbyterian minister, Eugene Adair, moved to New York where her husband pastored a new parish. Thelma completed her doctorate in Education at Teachers College, Columbia University.

She started a six-day weekly day-care program for children in Harlem, and became the director of Head Start Programs, a consultant and Professor of Education at Queens College, New York. She coordinated the education component of the Peace Corps and worked with projects in many countries in West Africa under the "Cross-Roads Africa" Program. She has authored several publications.

Thelma is a model and mentor for women of National Black Presbyterian Women (formerly United Presbyterian Women), and members of the National Black Presbyterian Caucus (formerly BPU).

A trademark of Thelma is her ability to tell stories in a way that personalizes them for deeper meanings.

Vera P. Swann
Moderator, National Black Presbyterian Women

I will give you shepherds after my own heart, who will lead you with knowledge and understanding.
Jeremiah 3:15 (NIV)

February 2007

Rev. Dr. Jeremiah A. Wright, Jr., Senior Pastor
TRINITY UNITED CHURCH OF CHRIST, Chicago, IL

Dearly beloved pastor and brother in Christ,
greetings and best wishes always!

We are highly honored by this privilege to salute you on this occasion.
Surely, for all who know of your tireless labors of love, in the name of Jesus,
our hearts overflow with joy as you are a Samuel DeWitt Proctor honoree.
Hallelujah!

For sure, the spirit of Dr. Proctor celebrates along with us. As one of your beloved mentees, many of us are aware of Dr. Proctor because you taught us about him. Thank you for "keeping on keeping on" and sharing your rich, God-given talents, teaching, preaching, singing and laboring in the vineyard. Thank you for showing and telling us what it means to be a servant leader. "Rev.," we thank and appreciate you for practicing what you preach, being a faithful steward, giving freely of your time, your talent and your treasure – all you have worked so hard to achieve.

We are blessed to have shared early years of ministry with you, as you worked 'til the day was done, striving to help us know the joy of being who God created us to be, Unashamedly Black and Unapologetically Christian; guiding us to be blessed by the knowledge of God's Word; teaching the old hymns of the Black church, helping us to appreciate and savor the privilege of being ministry partners and good stewards and so much more. For all of this, we can only shout – out loud – and/or in our hearts, "We thank you, Jesus! You let Pastor Wright bring us from a mighty long way!"

And because God is generous beyond description, you are blessed to not only serve our congregation faithfully, but God is blessing you to serve peoples everywhere! Many of them, as well as us, know first-hand about God's vast world because you personally carry "whosoever will" from here to the shores of Mother Africa, and other places many thought existed only in the day-dreaming minds of many writers. We are richly blessed by the knowledge and lessons of your worldview. God bless you for loving God's people whoever and wherever they are.

Blessings always. We love ya, man!
Joyfully, us Allens

S & B

Sam and Rev. Barbara
Jeremiah 3:15

A Tribute and Letter From the Heart

Rev. Dr. Jeremiah A. Wright, Jr.

Rev.,

When we first met at a fundraiser event for children, nearly thirty years ago, we both had big black Afros, we had read Cone, Clarke, Malcolm and King; we were on a journey full of vision, energy and expectation, Black, proud and Christian by training. I had been to Africa several times, and was armed with the vision of Bishop Henry McNeal Turner, the model of Mary McLeod Bethune and the poems of Carolyn Rodgers.

You were this affable, informed, laid back preacher who invited me, not to leave my church, but to volunteer at yours, a church with a denominational name unknown to me. You asked me to help with your vision for a school. I discovered at your church a worshiping congregation and a sacred space where being **"unapologetically black and unashamedly Christian"** was not seen as a contradiction. I found through you, a ministry and message that was not a sham or shameful.

When you retell the events surrounding your birth, it is clear you defied all odds and it was only by God's grace, mercy and will that you lived. But, not only did you live, you were divinely gifted with intellectual genius, creative sensibilities, passion and compassion. Your divine gifts were nurtured in a family tradition firmly rooted in Christian values, love of education and pride in one's identity. The rest is His story. It was ordained in your mother's womb.

I have seen you as a prophet in the watchtower, a theologian who preaches, an accomplished musician and prodigious wordsmith, editor and author, a scholar in multiple disciplines, a linguist who translates languages and cultures, an administrator and overseer who builds, sustains and delegates. One could even argue, God was partial!

And, yes, though I am still looking for your clones, you are human. You know what it means to be a son, a husband, a father, and a friend who loves, laughs, laments and is loyal.

You are my pastor, preacher, teacher, colleague, friend and "big" brother. We have shared sorrow and death, parenting and parents' stories, books and ideas, disappointments and despair, jokes and jubilation, organizational visions and challenges.

You consecrated my ministry with prayers in three different languages, representing three different continents. We have been down dusty roads throughout the world together where we ministered to and were ministered by those destined to die impoverished, yet holding on to their human dignity and belief in a righteous God. We have shared moments of silence and the compassion that comes with true and unconditional friendship.

My dear brother Jeremiah, you are a man of God who has seen very correctly. You walk with a transcendent faithfulness to the prophetic call on your life and your very being. Because of your faithfulness, many of your visions have been realized and your school is about to be built.

We learned that Jeremiah was the weeping prophet and a Jeremiad means a message of thunderous warning and profound hope. You have given us *The Audacity to Hope* and *The Day of Jerusalem's Fall.* Continue to stay in your prayer closet, bursting out with the next Jeremiad. And even when it might seem that you are alone, remember that weeping may endure for a night, but joy comes in the morning. With each and every sunrise, you are surrounded by those who have been indelibly convicted at the hands of your potter's wheel. You are a gift from God for such a time as this. We celebrate you now and forever more!

Dr. Iva E. Carruthers

BLESSED TO SHARE THE JOURNEY

Dr. Thelma Davidson Adair

*I*t was my good fortune to be among thirty-six educators selected to participate in a program entitled "Operation Crossroads Africa," organized by an African American Presbyterian minister for the purpose of working cooperatively with elementary school teachers in Liberia, West Africa, during the summer of 1962.

During orientation at Lincoln University in Pennsylvania, I was struck by the number of persons who were entering the dining room to speak to one of the teachers. Who was this red-haired woman with whom so many people wanted to chat? It was not long before I met her when she and four other women were assigned to the same cottage. I learned that she was Dr. Thelma Adair, a professor of early childhood education in New York City.

She was born and reared in South Carolina. At an early age she graduated from one of the African American colleges in North Carolina. After her marriage to the Rev. Dr. Eugene Adair, they moved to New York City where they purchased a three-story brownstone house. Their home was located in Harlem, where she lives to this day.

Over the years, my contacts with Thelma Adair have been numerous, including mutual home visits with our families, at Presbyterian gatherings and late night telephone calls, not to mention our shopping trips.

Dr. Adair's contributions to the Presbyterian Church have been legion as well as numerous. Among her many outstanding accomplishments are the following:

1.   First African American female moderator of the United Presbyterian Church in the U.S.A.
2.   Twice elected the national president of Church Women United
3.   Her extensive travels and lectures throughout the U.S.A. and the world

Her dedication to the education of young children continues to this day. As an octogenarian, she continues to use her experiences and talents with the Head Start Program of New York City.

Dr. Adair is the widow of the Rev. Dr. Eugene Adair, the mother of two sons, one daughter and the doting grandmother of five grandchildren and two great-grandchildren

I can truthfully say that, in my 83 years of life, she is the most brilliant, charismatic, caring and concerned woman that I have been fortunate to know.

Wilda C. Stephenson
Retired Asst. Professor
The University of Nebraska at Omaha

HUMILITY BEFORE HONOR

Dr. Thelma Davidson Adair

Sisters and Brothers:

You were witnessing a great moment in history if you were in Baltimore's convention hall on May 21, 1976, when the 188th General Assembly of the United Presbyterian Church presented the gavel to Dr. Thelma Davidson Adair, the first African American woman to be elected Moderator of the highest court of the church.

This was one of the most impressive and dramatic investitures in the history of the denomination because a huge throng of African Americans surrounded her on the stage, representing several generations of her husband's family of Adairs, who were Presbyterians before Emancipation, and of Davidsons, who were black Baptist members of the white North Carolina slaveholder family after whom Davidson College was named. It was a thrilling spectacle.

One of the most prominent church women in the nation, Thelma Adair, and her husband, Eugene, a Presbyterian minister and national missionary, pioneered child care and early childhood education in the 20th century. Their work at Mt. Morris Presbyterian Church in Harlem was a model for Head Start and other urban educational programs. After earning her Ph.D at Columbia, Thelma became a distinguished Professor of Education at Queens College, a consultant for the Peace Corps, UNESCO, and numerous universities. She has been a selfless mentor and contributor to large and small causes nationally and internationally.

Bryant George, her old friend and fellow J.C. Smith University alumnus, sums up Thelma's long career with this encomium: "She has been privileged to hold many top positions and has used them not to burnish her credentials but rather to help women and minorities to get ahead in both the church and the society." Thelma Davidson Adair, now an honorably retired Ruling Elder in her Harlem congregation, continues, by the grace of God, to be a peerless minister of the worldwide Church of Jesus Christ.

Gayraud S. Wilmore

I was a stranger and you welcomed me...
Matthew 25:35 (NRSV)

Dr. Thelma Davidson Adair

CHESTNUT, SANDERS, SANDERS, PETTAWAY & CAMPBELL, L.L.C.
ATTORNEYS AND COUNSELORS AT LAW
SELMA, ALABAMA

I was 17, southern, naïve but determined to live in Harlem U.S.A. The year was 1963. The South was preparing for a major non-violent revolution when I boarded a bus to New York City, determined not to spend the summer on Dynamite Hill in Birmingham, Alabama.

When I arrived in Harlem, I had no place to live. I was taken to the home of Dr. and Rev. Adair on 122nd, Mt. Morris. My reception was simply incredible. I, along with other students from Johnson C. Smith, slept in their beds, ate their food and paid no rent. Dr. Adair opened her home and her heart to young women from the South that she knew nothing about. She cared for us and gave us the aspiration to be our best selves. On the steps of Mount Morris Presbyterian Church, I learned how to organize, to lead and create music and plays.

The Adairs nurtured and allowed me space to grow and develop without any demands. I returned every summer between college and law school to their space where my blessings overflowed. These wonderful people taught me how to be a servant. Over the years scores of people have shared our home in Selma, Alabama.

I owe my education in life and at Johnson C. Smith University and Harvard Law School, in great part, to the Adairs. My gratitude is best demonstrated by my commitment to serve others as they served me.

Rose Sanders

VERNON E JORDAN JR

30 ROCKEFELLER PLAZA
NEW YORK NY 00?0

To the Samuel DeWitt Proctor Conference:

It is fitting and proper that Rev. Dr. Otis Moss, Jr. is being honored at the February 2007 Samuel DeWitt Proctor Conference. For Otis Moss, Jr. and Samuel DeWitt Proctor, though separated by age and time, have traveled similar paths. Both were born and reared in the Old South; attended segregated public schools; earned bachelor degrees from two of our best private black colleges, Virginia Union and Morehouse; at early ages taken by their parents to Baptist churches where they heard the deacon pray, the choir sing, the preacher preach and, like Isaiah, they "saw the Lord high and lifted up" and they never got over it. Both were activists in the civil rights movement, the Progressive National Convention, the United Negro College Fund and other organizations dedicated to equal justice and freedom.

Of particular interest to me is that I am the beneficiary, for many years, of a marvelous friendship with Proctor and Moss. They have provided counsel, comfort, support and spiritual guidance throughout my career. I have spoken to their congregations and provided pro bono counsel in their various stewardships.

Therefore, I have standing to have a word about Rev. Dr. Otis Moss, Jr. We met in the morning of our careers in Atlanta, where we were "soldiers in the Army." His beautiful and talented wife, Edwina, and I grew up together in the first public housing project for black people in America, University Homes. We finished elementary school in the same class. When I was shot in Indiana, Otis rushed to my bedside with prayer and encouragement. And he came to New York to participate in my first wife's homegoing. He is on call daily when I need a biblical reference for a speech or paper. He has taught me that "friendship is the medicine of life."

I am convinced that in an English Literature class at Morehouse, Otis read these words from Herman

Melville and was inspired and instructed by them:

> We cannot live for ourselves alone
> Our lives are connect by a thousand
> Invisible threads, and along these
> Sympathetic fibers our actions run as causes
> And return to us as results

Pastorships in Atlanta, Cincinnati, Cleveland, in addition to his nationwide preaching have established beyond any shadow of doubt that Otis Moss is one of America's most gifted preachers and successful pastors. Otis Moss is a whole preacher who preaches a full gospel as set forth in Luke 10:27:

> Thou shalt love the Lord thy God
> With all thy heart, and with all thy
> Soul, and with all thy strength, and with all
> thy mind; and thy neighbor as thyself.

Leader, scholar, educator, preacher, pastor, servant, husband, father, grandfather, friend – all define the life that Otis Moss lives and has lived ever since we joined in friendship. We are better people and a better nation because Otis Moss lives and works among us.

Otis Moss has earned the right to and richly deserves this recognition from the Samuel DeWitt Proctor Conference.

Sincerely,

Vernon E. Jordan, Jr.

THEN

Rev. Dr. James H. Cone

SCHOLAR, TEACHER, MENTOR, FRIEND

Rev. Dr. James H. Cone

"We don't need another James Cone." I remember these words as if you said them to me yesterday – instead of a few months prior to the beginning of my Ph.D. studies with you at Union Theological Seminary, New York. You must find your own voice. Years earlier, you certainly found your voice as the Father of Black Liberation Theology.

Your development of Black Liberation Theology demonstrates what happens when we are able to stand with integrity on the shoulders of our foreparents like Denmark Vesey, Richard Allen, Jarena Lee, Sojourner Truth, Harriet Tubman, Henry McNeil Turner and many others.

While at Union, I would smile softly when a graduate school friend would call me "Cone's Clone." He just didn't understand. Unlike leaders who dedicate themselves to producing "religious/theological robots," you, Jim Cone, have been dedicated to your ministry of scholarship and the production and/or enabling of scholars committed to justice and liberation of the Gospel.

You have produced some 40 or so persons (mostly persons of color) with the doctor of philosophy degree in theology. Their new voices are now heard in academic and ecclesial institutions around the world. Your teaching and writings have already had a tremendous reach on generations past and present, and will continue into the distant future.

You've been an encouraging and empowering teacher/scholar, by teaching your students not what to think, but how to think. You've been empowering as you've challenged people to ask the right questions --- even when they are controversial and uncomfortable.

Jim, you have enabled many to "find or to develop their own voices." With your article, "The Role of Women in Ministry: A Theological Appraisal," you provided gravely needed support for women as you challenged men invested in patriarchal privilege (even as they reject white privilege of white supremacy ideology).

It was not a one-shot-deal; it was not merely a fashionable thing to do; it was not just another speaking engagement; it was not a matter of keeping the women quiet and in their place. You were truly convinced that sexism is a sin to be eradicated, and this has been reflected in your work consistently.

You helped me to discover and to develop my own voice as you have done for many women scholars and women practitioners in church and other ministries.

Truly, you have modeled for men that it is not only possible to be pro-black liberation and pro-women's liberation at the same time, but that it is necessary, if real liberation is to be a reality.

You see, my friend in graduate school just didn't understand --- it's not about "cloning" it's about, "claiming, covenanting, challenging and commissioning."

When Good News is really Good, you can't keep it to yourself. You didn't keep it to yourself; you have empowered many women and men from the last 30 years of the 20th century through the present and into the future.

Many join me as I say – I am eternally and lovingly grateful.

Rev. Jacquelyn Grant, Ph.D.

Rev. Dr. James H. Cone

James H. Cone, an A.M.E. clergyman and systematic theologian, hails from Bearden, Arkansas. It was there that his theological passion for racial justice was forged. Growing up in a segregated society dominated by white Christian power over black people's struggle for survival and freedom, Cone was nurtured by the faith of the black church and an intellectual curiosity to bring reason to bear on belief. The affirmation of the African American religious community and the encouragement of his family spurred Cone on to always seek excellence in whatever he chose to do. Indeed, he accepted the call to ministry at the age of 16. It is the gospel of Jesus Christ – the cross and resurrection – that fires Cone's passion for a theological understanding of a new earthly vision, one free of racism, poverty, and all forms of inhumane social relations. To accomplish this task, Cone has consistently posed the question for people of faith: What is critical reflection on the nature of the divine calling? Is the church accountable to the One who proclaimed that "the Spirit of the Lord is upon me"? For several decades, Cone has adhered to that calling by following the Way of Jesus as the Crucified One who stands in solidarity with the poor.

Dr. Cone continues the black tradition of prophetic faith seeking intellectual understanding. He earned a B.A. from Philander Smith College (Little Rock, Arkansas), B.D. from Garrett Theological Seminary, and a M.A. from Northwestern University. He is the first African American to graduate from the Ph.D. program from Northwestern University. He has at least 10 honorary degrees and 12 books translated into Dutch, German, Japanese, Korean, Italian, Spanish, Portuguese, Malayalam (India), and French. He began his teaching career in 1964 at Philander Smith College (an A.M.E. school). From September 1969 to the present, Cone has been at Union Theological Seminary (New York City) where currently he holds the coveted title, Charles A. Briggs Distinguished Professor of Systematic Theology.

Dr. Cone has achieved what few human beings have done. He created a new discipline, a pioneering body of writing, and a systematic theology. At least in three ways, he accomplished this goal. First, he wrote the initial book on black theology of liberation. In fact, evidence suggests that the March 1969 publication of his Black Theology and Black Power was the first text on liberation theology in the world. As a result, a son of the black church was one of the founders of liberation theology on the earth. About a dozen books have followed, leading to his current project that compares the cross and lynching. In addition to book publications, Cone globalized black theology of liberation through his many international networks. Every continent and all habitable islands are aware of the gift of black theology coming from the black church. And third, Cone produced 3 generations of younger scholars as he now grooms a fourth one.

Can anything good come out of Bearden? Yes, look what God has done! Who would have ever imagined that from the cotton picking fields of Arkansas has arisen a man who has lectured at over 800 colleges, universities, divinity schools, and community organizations in the United States; directly impacted Steve Biko and the Black Consciousness Movement in apartheid South Africa; is an A.M.E. preacher and former pastor; authored about 200 articles; trained many of the 1st and 2nd generations of womanist preachers and professors; graduated many of the church leaders in Africa, Asia, the Caribbean, and Latin America; received the prestigious American Black Achievement Award in the category of religion given by Ebony Magazine; is the subject of Master theses, Ph.D. dissertations, and published books; taught several generations of African American church pastors.

Yes, someone good has come out of Bearden, Arkansas – James Hal Cone – son of the church, father of black theology; servant of the international poor, and a witness of Jesus Christ the Liberator.

Rev. Dr. Dwight N. Hopkins

Rev. Dr. James H. Cone

Dearest Dr. Cone:

You are, without a doubt, "a teacher sent from God" to both inspire and challenge the Church, Society and the Academy, compelling them to places they perhaps would never have gone, but for the fact that God made you a force of nature, uniquely so! I want you to know that I continuously reflect on your life and public witness, and the meaning of our time together.

As a young seminarian, I thought I needed you to cultivate my militancy; yet the deeper lessons you taught me made me freer and more hopeful than I believed possible. Now, as a still-fledgling theologian, I recognize you as a gracious gift, the Teacher who led me to the fullest appreciation of my place in the struggle for human liberation. Thank you for recognizing me as your student, for befriending me, mentoring me and giving me opportunity to explore my vocation and realize the truth of my somebodyness. Thank God you have done so for me and for everyone whom you mentor, who read your books and otherwise encounter your spirit and fire!

I hold you in the highest loving regard, and always will.

Faithfully yours,

Rev. JoAnne Marie Terrell, Ph.D.

TODAY

Rev. Dr. James H. Cone

Sr. Francesca Thompson, CSF

Dear Francesca,

In the course of the fourteen years we have been colleagues, it has been my happy duty to congratulate you on a fairly regular basis for the extraordinary range of honors you have received during that time. Therefore, I hope you will not mind if I tell you I was not really surprised when I heard that the Samuel DeWitt Proctor Conference had named you one of the recipients of the awards it sponsors honoring "giants who, by their gifts and labors, have secured a place in our hearts in history." Therefore, on behalf of the entire Fordham family (all of whom are happy to bask in your reflected glory), I would like to congratulate you on this latest well-earned and richly deserved recognition of the remarkable contributions you have made to the life of both our beloved University and the nation.

On a far more personal and local level, Francesca, I would also like to thank you for all that you have done and continue to do for Fordham. When you first stepped foot on the Rose Hill campus, you took the place by storm--for reasons that are easy to understand. As a teacher, you have challenged your students to dream great dreams and to move beyond the limits they wrongly believed they had when they arrived on campus. As an advocate, you have transformed the lives not only of your students, but also of your faculty colleagues. As a preacher, you have brought the Word of God alive with the force and passion of the prophets. As a friend, you have been unstinting in the support you have given all who have been fortunate enough to know you. In short, you have been both a force of nature and a giant in the Fordham community. For my part, I must tell you that I have always been impressed by the breadth of your knowledge, the depth of your love for the mystery of God's presence in the world, and the passion and focus with which you have lived out your religious vocation. We at Fordham are more proud than we could ever say of all that you have done for the University, and immensely grateful for the transforming gift of your presence in our midst.

May God our Lord continue to make you an instrument of transforming grace for all who know you.

Sincerely,

Joseph M. McShane, S.J.
President
Fordham University

A Wise Woman Builds Her House
Proverb 14:1a

Dr. Thelma Davidson Adair

I would like to thank the Samuel DeWitt Proctor Conference for this opportunity to share the deep love and respect that I have for my mother, Dr. Thelma C. Adair.

The text of my Father's last sermon was "As a mother comforts her child, so I will comfort you." - Isaiah 66:13. I think he chose this text because, in part, he had seen the motherly love that Thelma C. Davidson Adair has shown her children: Robert, Jeanne, and Richard, and her grandchildren: Kai, Aton, Clarence, Osei, Barbara Jean, Alexandra, and Ross.

Mother is not perfect (can she cook?) but, as Daddy said, "She doesn't have a mean bone in her body." She is generous to a fault, thoughtful, kind, smart as heck, shrewd, strategic, daring, and she has a wicked sense of humor. She is a person for all ages. To see "Dr. Reindeer" interact with young children is humbling.

I share this story with my students. The day that Mother received her doctorate from Columbia University, Teachers College, I remember reflecting on the late nights and early mornings that she had devoted to her thesis (no computer or white-out) after a day of work-work, church-work and caring for us. I remember her standing in her doctoral gown and being hooded and my thinking, "You can't buy that outfit; you have to earn it."

For me, Mother has been a ceaseless source of love, care, and inspiration. I shall always hear Mother saying, "I think you did wonderfully or go on, you can do it." I can't remember her discouraging me from any challenge from being a mother to earning a doctorate.

I thank God for giving me Thelma C. Davidson Adair as a mother, a mentor, a friend, a wise counsel, and an outstanding example of a SBW (Strong Black Woman).

~Jeanne Davidson Adair, Daughter

A Grandmother's Faith and Love

Dr. Thelma Davidson Adair

First and foremost, I would have to say that my grandmother has and will always be a constant source of praise and confidence in my life. There is nothing her grandchildren cannot do, and she has never failed to remind us of this. An unending source of encouragement and influence, she not only encourages our hopes and endeavors but leads by example with her constant commitment to her faith, family and community. I have known her as a nurturer, a leader and friend, and I am pleased and excited that she is being recognized for what she continues to give to so many.

I love you Grandma,

~Barbara Jean Adair

One thing that I have always admired about my grandma is her courage. Every time I go to a banquet or any event honoring her, I learn something new about what she has done not only for the community, but for our family as well. From her courage in starting the headstart centers all over New York, to her courage in moderating the Presbyterian Church, to her courage in raising three children, my Grandmother has done it all with no fear. But not only that, my Grandma has shared this adventurous side of her with me and both of my sisters. I remember our trips to Martha's Vineyard and Milwaukee, where Grandma was never afraid to go anywhere or do anything. To have such a courageous and fearless grandmother has inspired me to never be afraid of trying new things. With all the wondrous places grandma has been to, the world doesn't seem as overwhelming. Now anyplace on the globe is opened up for me through her experiences, and I will cherish that for the rest of my life.

Love you Grandma,
~Ross Adair

Dr. Thelma Davidson Adair

My grandmother has always been a great inspiration in my life. I have always admired her work and her drive, and always tried to apply that in my own life. I will never forget when she took me to Puerto Rico for one of her conventions. I was about 10, and it was one of the most memorable experiences in my life. On that trip I learned so many things about Puerto Rico; my grandmother made sure that I saw and experienced everything possible. Even though the trip was not a vacation for her, and she was still working, my grandmother made sure it was nothing but a vacation for me. That's who my grandmother is, a woman who is always working, while always thinking of others. I will never forget when we went in the forest and traveled up a tall mountain, from which we could see all of Puerto Rico; it was by far one of the prettiest sights that I have ever seen. In the forest there was a beautiful waterfall and my grandmother and I took many pictures in front of it. There was also a small village in the forest where people sold many trinkets. There my grandmother and I bought jewelry, which I still have today, to remember my wonderful trip with my grandmother. My trip to Puerto Rico was only one of many times that my grandmother has done something memorable in my life. She is always teaching and caring for me. Now that I am older, I appreciate everything she does so much more, and recognize what a strong and amazing woman she is.

~**Alexandra Elizabeth Adair**

As I await the arrival of my first child, I reflect upon learned life lessons and their relevancy to my unborn child. This reflection requires meaningful consideration of my grandmother, Dr. Thelma D. Adair, and the many lessons she taught my brother, Osei, and me.

Her teachings emphasized spiritual, physical and intellectual achievement. With these lessons she sought to make us ready and able to take on the complex issues of morality, health, faith and education that characterize our local, national and global communities today. Her model of hard work equating to excellence, intellectual ability defining opportunity, and spiritual and physical health translating to wholeness were evident at all times. They in fact were the hallmarks of her effective and principled leadership. What's more they inspired a generation of men and women throughout the world to be great and work for positive change.

Our Grandmother's life lessons and her leadership represent a solid, ethical and lasting legacy for my brother and me, as well as many young leaders of today and in the future, to embrace and follow. Osei and I, and our wives, Courtney and Darly, wish Grandmother the best and greatest gratitude for excellence as a person, leader and her unwavering commitment to us and family.

~**Clarence Eugene and Osei Jean-Louis Mevs**

FAMILY

Dr. Thelma Davidson Adair

SPIRIT WITHOUT LIMIT

Sr. Francesca Thompson, OSF

I first met Evelyn (Francesca) Thompson when we both attended St. Mary Academy. Blessed with a healthy self-image, Evelyn quickly overcame hesitance, if not prejudice, by her real appreciation for people. As a result she had many friends in a school that was 95 percent white. She shared her talent for giving monologues before the student body, which many remember (especially me) with appreciation and awe to this day. Her love of the theatre became evident during those years.

I again met up with her when we entered the Sisters of St. Francis, Oldenburg where I got to know her better, causing my admiration for her to grow. She loved the Community and each sister in it, never failing to let others know that she was a Franciscan Sister.

Again we were together at Marian College where she taught in the Theatre Department and directed plays. Do you know many play directors who could be in the lobby ten minutes before the play began, circulating among the patrons, and have the play begin on time? I KNOW ONE! Although she is an artist, she is an organized one who expected her students and actors to meet her expectations. I suspect that she continued these traits and expectations when she attended graduate school and in her teaching at Fordham University. Through her many years in New York, she never lost touch with who she is - a Franciscan Sister from Oldenburg--nor with the members of our community.

You are and will always be an Oldenburg Franciscan! Thank you, Francesca, for our friendship.

Sr. Marilynn Hofer, OSF
Assistant Alumni Director
Marian College
Indianapolis, IN

Sr. Francesca Thompson, OSF

A JEWEL IN THE CROWN

Rev. Dr. Otis Moss Jr.

Otis Moss, Jr. has been my friend, colleague, confidante and ministry neighbor for twenty years. He preached a memorable sermon at my installation as pastor at Antioch Baptist Church in Cleveland. I have preached the ordination sermon for at least six of his sons and daughters in the ministry. He wrote either the foreword or an endorsement in two of my books. We exchange pulpits on a regular basis; although I know that the better blessing always occurs when he is the preacher. We work hand-in-hand in our local clergy fellowship; United Pastors in Mission. He and I walked the halls of the United States Senate Office Building together back in 1990 trying to persuade members of the Senate Judiciary Committee not to confirm Clarence Thomas to the U.S. Supreme Court. That is one effort concerning which most Americans now wish we had been successful. We have been colleagues and friends for twenty years.

Many people may know him better at the national level, but nobody has a better sense than I of the true scope and reach of his ministry here at home. His stature in Cleveland is very nearly "heroic" in the Greek mythology sense of the word. His influence reaches in every direction and into every sector of our community. His opinion is sought out on all matters of public life. His preaching is eagerly anticipated and happily heard. We in Cleveland already know that Rev. Dr. Otis Moss, Jr. is a jewel in the crown of Jehovah. We salute him on this occasion of his recognition in memory of our mutual mentor, Dr. Samuel Dewitt Proctor.

The Rev. Marvin A. McMickle, Ph.D.
Pastor of Antioch Baptist Church
Cleveland, OH

Rev. Dr. Otis Moss Jr.

Rev. Dr. Jeremiah A. Wright, Jr.

My Dearest Brilliant, Benevolent, Bay' Brotha:

"I can do all things through Christ who strengthens me."

Phillipians 4:13

I thank God for placing us in each others lives and providing 20th Century technology to shorten the communication miles between us. While traveling globally each year, educating and reviving thousands, you gallantly direct our growing congregation with extraordinary vision and passion. For years I have wondered **how** you could be so knowledgeable/multi-lingual, do so much while still being a fantastic husband, father, mentor and more!

Finally, through Philippians 4:13, I realized that it wasn't you doing too much ... it was God doing so much through you!

Now you're being honored among the "Giants in The Industry," by the Samuel DeWitt Proctor Conference. How appropriate, since you are the Goliath of ministerial messengers! From the first sermon I heard you preach, **"What Makes You So Strong?" (10/8/89)**, my eyes were opened to the magnificence of your teaching while preaching powerfulness! Sermon after sermon, your scripture references are skillfully infused into today's cultural/personal/political realities. And whether you're singing a Long Meter hymn or "du-wops," I'm smiling, remembering ... relating!

B4, I cherish the bountiful blessings you've placed in my life! Through the years, sharing our home with you, Ramah and Jamila has been a joy. Not only do you lift my name in prayer each week, you never forget my birthday or my family's health concerns! **I praise God for "doing so much through you,"** knowing your will ...

Keep Looking Up,

Cynthia - Christian

HIS EYE IS ON THE SPARROW

Sr. Francesca Thompson, OSF

Only the most unusual doctoral students would describe their dissertation as a labor of love, but surely none would do so in the same sense as Sister Francesca Thompson, when she pursued her doctorate in theater at the University of Michigan at Ann Arbor thirty years ago. The topic of her dissertation was The Lafayette Players, founded in 1915 as the first Black dramatic stock company in the United States. Sister Francesca's parents, Edward Thompson and Evelyn Preer, were prominent members of The Lafayette Players. Both had worked on the legitimate stage and in the silent movies of the day. Evelyn Preer died in 1932, seven months after giving birth to their only child, a daughter who would later enter the community of the sisters of St. Francis of Oldenburg and henceforth be known as Sister Francesca.

After receiving her doctorate from the University of Michigan, Sister Francesca was chair for eight years of the Department of Theater and Speech at her alma mater, Marion College in Indianapolis. In 1982, she joined the Fordham University community as Associate Professor in Afro-American Studies and the Department of Communications and Assistant Dean for Minority Affairs. As teacher, director and mentor, she has been the advocate and inspiration of several generations of Fordham men and women, to whom she has imparted a love of the theater and the confidence that they will realize their dreams with God's help since "His eye is on the sparrow and I know He still watches over me!"

A compelling speaker, Sister Francesca has lectured at universities and religious conferences across the nation. The breadth of her activities can be glimpsed in the contributions she has made not only as a member of the National Black Sister's Conference, but also as a member of the Tony Awards Committee. With gratitude for her service to Fordham and in celebration of her Golden Anniversary as a sister of St. Francis, Fordham University bestowed on Sister Francesca Thompson the degree of Doctor of Fine Arts at the 2002 University Commencement.

Jeffrey Gray
Vice President, Student Affairs
Fordham University

Dr. Thelma Davidson Adair

*I*n the early 70's, while studying at Union Theological Seminary in New York City, I read about Dr. Thelma and her late husband, Rev. Adair; they had returned from Ghana on an educational trip. Being a Ghanaian, I could not help but make my way to meet the Adairs.

For over thirty years, Dr. Thelma Adair has been known to me and most Africans, especially Ghanaian national residents in the Metropolitan area, as very active in her church. I am honored and privileged to participate in the special celebration of honour in gratitude for her many years of outstanding, inspirational and untiring dedication and commitment in serving God and others.

Since 1973, I've been a member of Mt. Morris Ascension Presbyterian Church in Harlem, New York. Thelma's leadership in all areas is significant and her contributions to make others' lives better are endless. She has assisted Mt. Morris Ascension Church Social Services with its development and implementation in numerous programs. Her work included sharing life skills workshops with teen mothers and families in temporary housing, hunger prevention, community education for self-dependency and early childhood education for parents and teachers.

After my theological studies, the Adairs encouraged the church to sponsor me for my permanent resident visa so that I would be able to stay in the U.S. I was ordained to take charge of the newly founded Presbyterian Church of Ghana in New York City. In May of 1990, with the leadership of Dr. Adair, 40 African Americans of Mt. Morris Ascension decided to visit Ghana. The group was made up of Dr. Thelma Adair (Leader), Eunice P. Rydings, Olivia William, Emma Pitts, Vernett Kennedy, Marian Taitt and others.

The team paid a courtesy call to the Moderator of the Presbyterian Church, Ghana. Thelma presented three new air conditioners to the church on behalf of the visitors. Members of the visiting team were taken to various congregations for worship. The visitors had a real moving experience to witness and feel African spirituality. In addition, the team had the opportunity to attend the Synod of the Presbyterian Church, Ghana. At the Synod, Dr. Thelma Adair gave a gift of a suitcase of medicine worth about $5,000.

Thelma, for your devoted, untiring and conscientious efforts in supporting and promoting the religious welfare of the Ghanaian Community in the United States and the Presbyterian Church, Ghana, please accept my hearty congratulations. I wish you all the best in all your endeavors to make others learn from you, even during your restful and enjoyable retirement days.

God's Blessings Upon You,
Rev. Dr. Francis Kumi Dwamena (Pastor Retired)
Presbyterian Church of Ghana in New York City

A Quintessential Black Theologian As Practitioner

Rev. Dr. Jeremiach A. Wright, Jr.

If James H. Cone is the quintessential Black theologian as academician, then Jeremiah A. Wright, Jr. is the quintessential Black theologian as practitioner. Although he never formally studied with Cone, he is perhaps the finest individual example of contemporary Black theology in practice. As a dynamic preacher, a beloved pastor, an awesome teacher, a noted scholar, a passionate social activist, and even an accomplished musician, no one else combines so many gifts and talents so effectively in the interest of Black liberation. And as the long-term senior pastor of the renowned Trinity United Church of Christ in Chicago, Illinois, he has silenced the skeptics of Black theology by demonstrating its relevance to the Black Church and the African American community. Among his abundant qualities are his brilliance, his commitment, his accessibility, and his humor.

Jerry's brilliance is undeniable. An avid reader, a critical thinker, and an eloquent communicator, his command of information, his analysis of issues, and his articulation of his views make him either an invaluable ally or a formidable adversary, depending on one's perspective. Either way, his ideas—even when controversial or unpopular—are highly respected because of their grounding in careful study, serious reflection, and thoughtful deliberation. Commitment is another one of Jerry's qualities. Outstanding are his commitments to people of African descent and to the gospel of Jesus Christ. Long before it was popular, "theologically correct," or, in the minds of some, even possible to be both Black and Christian at the same time, he led the members of his congregation to boldly proclaim that they were "unashamedly Black and unapologetically Christian."

One of Jerry's most remarkable attributes is his accessibility. As a busy pastor, responsible for thousands of parishioners and, at the same time, in great demand as a preacher and speaker throughout the world, it is amazing that he has never lost the personal touch. Some way, somehow, he continues to make everyone he meets—and, especially, the members of Trinity—feel as if their problems are his problems and that he is never too busy to care about, or respond to, their individual needs and concerns. Last, but not least, Jerry is known for his humor. He is a natural jester and story teller (he got it honest—from his Mom) who can turn any situation—no matter how sacred or grave—into a lighthearted (and sometimes irreverent) moment of laughter and comic relief.

Jerry, what a delight it is for me to pause to say, "Thank you." (You see, I can call him "Jerry" because he is my cousin.) Thank you, cuz, for just being you. For you are a blessing to Black people, the church, and the world. And even though you do get on my nerves sometimes ("You're still wrong, man!"), I love you, I thank God for you, and I am proud to claim you as a member of my family.

Dennis W. Wiley, Ph.D.

ADVOCATE JUSTICE

Dr. Thelma Davidson Adair

I know Dr. Thelma Adair as a church leader, resource person, colleague and friend. She grew up in a Christian family. In her daily life she has always stood as a witness to her faith and has constantly been an inspiration to others.

She has always given the best of herself in the service of the Lord. Thelma has brought rich gifts to her various roles in the church and "Society-at-Large." Her ecumenical awareness and involvement in mission and leadership development have been outstanding! Her educational background assisted in developing Christian Education with a focus for Black Americans. She and her husband, the Rev. Dr. Eugene Adair, now deceased, developed an outstanding nursery and other educational programs at his church in New York City.

Thelma has traveled extensively and understands other cultures as she continues to be a student of world diversity. We have benefited from her organizational skills. She communicates well, but she also listens well. Thelma is sensitive to the needs of all people and their struggles. She is a strong advocate for justice!

Her leadership in the Presbyterian Church (USA) has been extraordinary. In 1976 at the 188th General Assembly of the United Presbyterian Church, she was elected Moderator. This was exceptional because she is an Elder and not a Minister; she is also a Black woman! As a friend, I remember how some of us gathered after her victory and really rejoiced!! She touched many lives in this position and continued to stress "women's issues and social justice."

Thelma and I shared meaningful dialogue with our friend, Mildred Brown, now deceased, who organized and developed the Third World Women Coordinating Team. She is never too busy to show that she cares about others. I remember how she comforted me in 1992, after my husband, Edgar W. Ward, former Director of the PCUSA's Vocation Unit had died. Although he had been dead six months, I was still in pain. She and I were attending the National Black Presbyterian Caucus and I was having difficulty because that was the first meeting I had attended without Edgar. She was a great comfort and blessing to me during that conference as I struggled with my grief.

Thelma worked hard in the Civil Rights Movement within our church. She served as president of Black Presbyterians United, President of Church Women United, worked with National Council of Churches and served as a member of the Presbyterian Interracial Council during the 60s and 70's. She is an articulate speaker regarding the history of Blacks in the Presbyterian Church, USA.

I respect and salute her!

Marjorie J. Ward
Retired Officer of the General Assembly, USA

GOD'S KINGDOM MAKER

Rev. Dr. Jeremiah A. Wright Jr.

I SALUTE YOU-- MY PASTOR, MY BROTHER, MY MENTOR AND MY FRIEND!

*I*count myself as truly blessed to have been associated with you since 1974. I appreciated all the welcoming warmth and friendship that you and your First Lady, and your precious daughters Janet and Jeri, extended to me as an outsider in a foreign land; that made me regard all of you as a precious part of my family, no matter where my God pilgrimage took me in this country. This precious feeling about all of you has prevailed in me to this very day. Praise God! "Through it all" you have prevailed as the firm foundation blocks for the benefits that thousands now enjoy from Trinity United Church of Christ (TUCC). Truth be told, these have resulted from your enduring faith, tough toil, trials and tribulations. Hallelujah!!!

You are truly an anointed man of God, who is called by many names that denote your God-given legendary character and anointing. I will only paint a brief sketch of these names, beginning with the prophetic name my own late father. The Rev. R. ZB .NGCOBO, sight unseen, called you HIS WARRIOR, THIS SIDE OF THE WATERS. This name was prophetic because my father also saw your kingship character, and you as kingdom maker for God. We Africans believe that one has to be an anointed warrior to truly be an effective king. This you truly are. You have gracefully prevailed as WARRIOR and KINGDOM MAKER for Christ through your exceptional shepherding leadership of Trinity United Church of Christ exemplified in TUCC's worldwide powerful witness as being UNASHAMEDLY BLACK AND UNAPOLOGETI-CALLY CHRISTIAN.

It was truly uplifting to us SOUTH AFRICANS to experience your tenacious warrior spirit in your "FREE SOUTH AFRICA" sign that prophetically stood out demanding, as well as prophesying, a reality that my spirit truly and prayer-fully believed the God of all possibilities would surely usher in. Thank you for standing with me/us. We South Africans call you "Vulindlela," which means way opener; it also means path finder. Your warrior influence has lived on transcending colour, culture, faith, denomination and distance. As a God kingdom builder, you have established a visible kingdom model. Trinity's phenomenal growth models competent and responsible leadership as well as develops leadership through continuous education and training as exemplified in your mentorship of ministers in training, and your fostering maintenance of ministries throughout the whole church.

Thanks for the major role that you and TUCC played in my ordination to God's Worldwide Ministry. Thanks for allowing God's mystery through that fiery event to break the decades of yokes and strongholds of resistance, so that the women of colour internationally could break forth with full authority. You made space for God to deliver through Trinity all the way to A.C.P.E. circle, in mysterious ways that keep on manifesting.

May we, who celebrate your tremendous anointing and giftedness recognize Christ, the solid foundation from which you continue to spring. We say to you, "continue to be God's mountain-moving musician; continue to be a Preacher, continue to cut through the mess, continue to be a speaker and challenging prophet." We love you. Be God's blessed eagle all the way!!

This tribute not only comes from me, but also on behalf of all the daughters and sons of Baba Rev. Zinda Rageson and Mama Zodwua Constance Ngcobo, and all South Africans you have touched in these ways.

Amen, Makubenjalo!!!
Reverend Dr. Thanda Ngcobo

Rev. Dr. Jeremiah A. Wright, Jr.

A GIFT FOR ALL GENERATIONS!

Rev. Dr. Jeremiah A. Wright, Jr.

I met Jeremiah Wright in the fall of 1988 while I was a student at Princeton Theological Seminary. I spent ten years on Wall Street prior to seminary, so I was carrying around a good bit of the arrogance that crass experience engenders. Jeremiah was scheduled as the featured preacher at the Princeton Seminary chapel that evening, and the Association of Black Seminarians was excitedly hosting him at a formal dinner before the service. All week my fellow students had raved so loudly and emotionally about this supposedly great preacher that I was sure he was yet another pulpit entertainer who whipped folks into a frenzy by talking loud and saying nothing. So I decided that at the dinner I would challenge him with carefully crafted questions that I was sure would cut him down to size.

At the dinner Jeremiah spoke briefly, then agreed to take questions. I couldn't wait to get at him. I rose and I threw both barrels at him with all the second-year seminarian erudition I could muster. Then I sat back down, fully satisfied that I had put this supposed-to-be great preacher in his place. Well, if Howard Cosell had been there he would have called it a drubbing. Seldomly in my life have I taken a greater intellectual beating. When Rev. Dr. Jeremiah Wright, Jr. finished with me, he had so thoroughly dismantled and discredited my arguments and made me look so bad – deservedly so, I must admit – that all I could say was a weak "amen" and sit with a sheepish grin wondering what would have happened if he hadn't mercifully decided to take it easy on a poor fool who, obviously had no idea how formidable and accomplished and how worthy of approbation and respect Jeremiah Wright and his ministry were.

Several years later, while I was a professor at Drew University, I invited him to breakfast when he was in New Jersey preaching a revival at Elmwood Presbyterian Church. I reminded him that I was that arrogant seminarian who had made such a fool of himself at Princeton Seminary. We laughed heartily. Then he gave me a gift I will always treasure: though he was light-years ahead of me in experience and accomplishment, he spoke to me as a peer. That small and generous gesture has meant more to me than he could ever imagine. I have loved him and counted him as a friend ever since. I have only one critique, or maybe it is better termed an excited expectation: that upon his retirement from the pastorate, he will be even more empowered to share the extraordinary breadth of his knowledge, his intellectual ruminations and his uncompromising prophetic vision with the waiting world.

Jeremiah, my friend and my mentor, I see your soft and generous heart beneath the gruff exterior. I know that in your ministry and in your dedication to establish God's love and justice on earth as in heaven, you have felt every painful blow, yet you have never slowed and you have never backed down. My love and admiration for you know no bounds and will always abound. May you forever be blessed with every good thing.

Dr. Obery Hendricks

HERITAGE AND HOPE

Dr. Thelma Davidson Adair

It is my honor to pay tribute to my friend and partner in ministry. Thelma Adair has been "a woman for all seasons" throughout many seasons in educational and religious circles. She has been a teacher of excellence as she led by example; she has been an inspiration as she has demonstrated through her witness and service what it means to be a fearless leader. Thelma's encouragement of emerging leaders has catapulted many persons, especially African American women, to new vistas of service.

Her signature saying is "Grab the mike!" When she became titular head of the Presbyterian Church (U.S.A.) as moderator of the General Assembly three decades ago, her message of "heritage and hope" traveled with her throughout the global community. That message still resonates with the African American Presbyterian community and serves as the catalyst in 2007 for our celebration of 200 years of "heritage and hope" as part of the faith community of the Presbyterian Church (U.S.A.).

To God be the glory for Thelma Adair --our partner in ministry who continues to push us forward this day and all the days of our lives.

--Mary Grace Rogers

I first became aware of the name Dr. Thelma Adair in 1963. My position with the commission of Ecumenical Missions, with specific responsibilities for women's programs, was the work of Dr. Thelma Adair. Dr. Adair was an elegant person whose presence throughout the Presbyterian Church catapulted her into prominence. In 1978, she became the first African American woman to become moderator of the General Assembly.

Her work with Crossroads Africa with Jim Robinson was noted when President Kennedy acknowledged that Crossroads was the progenitor for the Peace Corps. Dr. Adair's educational work has continued as director of many early childhood programs. Dr. Adair, as academic dean, elevated two Presbyterian universities, Boggs and Mary Holems, to accreditation status.

I consider her walk as a friend and colleague a gift from God.

--Lillian Anthony

Rev. Dr. Otis Moss Jr.

Tribute to Otis Moss

Otis Moss is one of the nation's most distinguished African-American leaders. His voice is valued in the halls of Congress and in the streets of Cleveland, Ohio, his hometown. He is a man for all seasons and for all people.

Otis Moss, father and grandfather, has passed his preaching skills on to his son who carries his name, Otis Moss III. Young Otis is now pastor of Trinity United Church of Christ in Chicago. He was called to the pulpit by Jeremiah Wright, pastor to the lowly and the lofty. The values taught by Otis, Sr. will last.

Most of all, Otis is a friend who is true and can be trusted. He has the courage to step out in faith even when he knows his actions will be misunderstood. He has been a teacher to Cleveland's white leadership. He has never sacrificed his deeply held beliefs just to be accepted. He has challenged white power and has confronted black power, calling both communities to be carriers of the dream Martin Luther King, Jr. set before this nation.

Otis is one of a kind. May God continue to bless his ministry.

By Rev. Dr. Joan Brown Campbell

A DIVINE APPOINTMENT

Sr. Francesca Thompson, OSF

Sister Francesca Thompson has made a huge contribution to the Fordham University community, and as her colleague for 15 years, I am so pleased to know that she is being honored by the Samuel D. Proctor Conference! From a human perspective, Sr. Francesca came to Fordham back in 1982 to serve a one year term as Scholar-in-Residence. From a divine perspective, there is no difference between one year and twenty-four years (2 Peter 3:8)! And we praise God for that!

God's gifted servant had a special mission during those twenty-four years: "to comfort the afflicted and afflict the comfortable." Sr. Francesca was a great source of comfort and a loving and compassionate advocate for students of color who needed a friend or a shoulder to cry on. The Spirit of the Lord was upon her to bind up the broken-hearted and to share the good news that God is alive and that they could make their way to graduation day.

Sr. Francesca also afflicted the comfortable by lifting her voice against racism and discrimination on this campus, in the church, and in the world. We thank God for her prophetic spirit, and her fierce determination and consistent commitment to the cause of peace and justice.

We are also very grateful that even as Sr. Francesca traveled to lecture in places far and wide, that she also came home to us. The members of the Department of African and African-American Studies at Fordham University are honored to have been her colleague, and we join the Samuel D. Proctor Conference in saluting her for her faithful service!

Sincerely,

Rev. Mark L. Chapman, Ph.D.
Associate Professor and Chair of
African and African-American Studies

A Truth Sayer....A Chain Breaker

Rev. Dr. James H. Cone

"Beautiful Are The Feet."

How does one describe all that flows from the heart based on a relationship that has lasted 38 years? It was 38 years ago when I met the Reverend Dr. James Cone. When I met him I was a Ph.D. student at The University of Chicago's Divinity School.

Dr. Cone was on the Examining Committee for the Fund for Theological Education. He interviewed me as a possible candidate for a Rockefeller Fellowship. I met him the year after his first book was written (***Black Theology and Black Power***). I stood in awe of him then and I stand in awe of him today.

Just being in Jim's presence was (and still is) overwhelming. James Cone is a man who loves the Lord, who loves African people and who loves the truth! His commitment to honesty, integrity and the life of the mind are without par.

James Cone is a man who loves the Lord, who loves African people and who loves the truth!

He has guided the Ph.D. work of so many students that they are almost like that number that John wrote about in the Book of Revelation. They are a "number which no man can number."

Jim's speaking the truth in love has opened the eyes of an entire generation of believers. His work with the Ecumenical Association of Third World Theologians, his work with the Black Theology Project, his teaching at Union Theological Seminary and his lecturing all over this world have "lifted the veil" of ignorance that was placed over the eyes of Africans by white supremacists.

His awesome work and his critical scholarship have also pulled the covers off of the body of lies that shaped the Christian church for the past 500 years of white supremacy. Jim has done more than "protest," however. He has pushed believers to see the truth, to embrace the Christ and to be delivered from those chains that bind us mentally.

Dr. Cone's commitment and integrity have shaped my ministry. They have helped me to see how it is possible to hold together in dynamic tension the life of the mind and the life of the spirit. He has helped me to integrate Black Theology in my preaching, my pastoring and my personal life.

I owe Jim a debt I can never repay, so I take this time to say to him publicly, "Thank you, my Brother!"

Pastor Jeremiah A. Wright, Jr., Senior Pastor
Trinity United Church of Christ
Chicago, IL

Chairperson
Prof. Dr. T.K. John SJ
Phones.: 23943556,23947609.
e-mail : tkjohnsj@jesuits.net

Centre for Dalit/Subaltern Studies

(Community Contextual Communication Centre)

Director
Prof. Dr. James Massey
Phones: 55477502, 25341375
M-9868202269
e-mail: cdss@vsnl.net & cccc@eth.ne

Sah-Shakti Sadan, KH: 94/11,
P.O. Matiala Village, Uttam Nagar
New Delhi - 110 059
(Adjacent Dwarka Phase-1, Sector 3)

Sub: A Letter of celebration for Dr. Cone's Contribution to Liberation theologies

Dear Dr. Carruthers,

It is indeed a privilege to be asked to write this letter of celebration in honor of Dr. James Cone. Though I have not met Dr. Cone personally, yet I know him through his writings on "Black theology." In fact I happily will confess that he is the one who helped me to understand the nature and role of Black theology. In many ways his thoughts have helped me to form my own thoughts on Dalit theology. It is true, Black theology and Dalit theology have been born from the two most suffering wombs (contexts) of the world, yet both of them share common concern for the liberation of black and dalit peoples. In support of what I have said here, I am quoting below two passages, one from Dr. Cone's essay and the other from my own essay. The passage from Dr. Cone is:

> Black Theology places our past and present actions toward black liberation in a theological context… The significance of Black Theology lies in the conviction that the content of the Christian gospel is liberation ... To speak of the God of Christianity is to speak of him who has defined himself according to the liberation of the oppressed. Christian theology … is the discipline that analyses the meaning of God's liberation in the light of Jesus Christ, showing that all actions that participate in the freedom of man are indeed the actions of God. (in *Black Theology-The South African Voice,* edited by Basil Moone, 1973, pp. 52,53)

The passage from my essay is:

> One important point to be noted here is that the term 'Dalit', when added as a prefix to 'theology', serves as a pointer to the role of … Dalit theology. The term 'Dalit' refers to the 'state' in which the people qualifying themselves by this term are living... Their history has helped them to know about their past lost identity ... how their singularity has been destroyed … This insight won by the Dalits forced them to engage themselves in the quest for 'solidarity' ... But finally it is the Dalit theology which is … placing the various actions of the past and the present in a theological context, as an assurance of what they have been or are doing right in the sight of God... (in *Yearbook of Contextual Theologies,* Missio, Aachen, Germany 2000, pp. 47, 48).

Now if one read carefully these two passages together, one may either hear some echoes of influence on thoughts and expressions or may find some close similarities between the two liberation theologies. Black theology being the older sister of Dalit theology certainly has influenced doing theology from the oppressed people's perspective. This relationship brings Dr. Cone not only nearer to Dalits of India, but also makes him partners in our struggle of the liberation.

May God continue to use Dr. James Cone mightly for God's people service.

Dated: 4th Dec. 2006
New Delhi, India

Prof. Dr. habil. James Massey,
Director, Centre for Dalit/Subaltern Studies

THE TRUE TRUTH

Sr. Francesca Thompson, OSF

Salutations to Sister Francesa Thompson OSF, teacher, dramatist, author, director, speaker and administrator. Whether addressing the Leadership Conference of Women Religious as their first African American key-note speaker, or the National Black Catholic Congress, she spoke the "true truth" with eloquence, erudition, humor and conviction. Through the years, Sister Francesca received countless awards and accolades. The medallion that she received in memory of the Venerable Pierre Toussaint from the Office of Black Ministry of the Archdiocese of New York summarizes who she is as a person: one, who furthers "… freedom, human rights and spiritual values in the Black Community" and beyond. This she does with "Franciscan Joy." I praise and thank my God for the gift of her friendship.

Sister Loretta Theresa
Fransiscan Handmaids of Mary

Sr. Francesca Thompson, OSF

FREDERICK G. SAMPSON
F O U N D A T I O N

*T*he Frederick G. Sampson Foundation and the Sampson Family are pleased to join with the Samuel DeWitt Proctor Conference in the celebration of the life and great works of Dr. Jeremiah Wright, Jr. He is a man of God, committed to the people of God, doing the work of God.

Dr. Wright has been an inspiration to the world as a visionary committed to meet people where they are and lift them up through spiritual enlightenment, cultural empowerment and social engagement. Throughout the years of doing the African American Male Spirituality Conference in Detroit, Dr. Wright would inspire people from all walks of life drawing thousands to hear him as he critiqued the culture, challenged cynicism and compelled us to Christ of the cross. He explains, engages, explores and enlightens us to experience spiritual eternity.

Personally, Dr. Wright stands in the intimate circle of great humanitarians and anointed men who have influenced my life. I call him friend, but more importantly, in the physical absence of my father, I call Dr. Wright my "Father Figure" – Daddy J. I stand in remembrance of a friendship between two men that transcends time and triumphs eternity as it continues to touch lives globally. I know that ministry is presence and he has over so many years exhibited his ministry in my life by both his profound homiletic gifts and by his ability to personally touch and be present. I celebrate this great man of God and this great friend of man.

He is unashamedly black and unapologetically Christian and extraordinarily visionary, strengthening, empowering and transforming God's people through his faith and actions. God bless you, Dr. Wright, and thank you.

Blessings,
Freda G. Sampson

736 LOTHROP AVENUE   DETROIT, MICHIGAN 48202
(313) 875 5230 T   (313) 875 5230 F
WWW.FGSFOUNDATION.ORG

United Church of Christ

February 5, 2007

The Collegium of Officers

John H. Thomas
General Minister and President

Edith A. Guffey
Associate General Minister

M. Linda Jaramillo
Justice and Witness Ministries

José A. Malayang
Local Church Ministries

Cally Rogers-Witte
Wider Church Ministries

Sisters and Brothers in Christ:

It is both an honor and a privilege to lift up in gratitude to God the faith, life, and witness of Dr. Jeremiah A. Wright, Jr. On behalf of the United Church of Christ I want to express our appreciation to the Samuel DeWitt Proctor Conference for honoring Dr. Wright for his leadership within and beyond the United Church of Christ.

Dr. Wright is one of the premier preachers in our land today, articulating the Gospel of Jesus Christ with compelling energy and prophetic urgency. To be in Trinity United Church of Christ is to be in the presence of the Word that comforts and consoles, challenges and confronts. His voice embodies Isaiah's words that name this award, "how beautiful upon the mountains are the feet of those who publish glad tidings, who promise peace."

For almost thirty-five years Dr. Wright has been building up the Body of Christ through his remarkable leadership of Trinity United Church of Christ, through his mentoring of countless young leaders in ministry, and through the planting of new congregations that Trinity has sponsored across our church. Know that as your Conference confers this distinguished award, a great cloud of witnesses across the United Church of Christ will join in celebration and thanksgiving.

Sincerely,

John H. Thomas
General Minister and President

700 Prospect Avenue, Cleveland, Ohio 44115-1100 ~ 866.822.8224 ~ Web www.ucc.org

93

ADVOCATE FOR STUDENTS

Sr. Francesca Thompson, OSF

What a privilege and a pleasure it is for me to acknowledge the significance of Sister Francesca Thompson to Fordham University and to me personally. Sister Francesca first came to Fordham in 1992 when I was serving as Department Chair. The search committee and administration were amazed by her knowledge, experience and passion. She made an immediate and lasting impact on the Fordham community as an Associate Professor in the African American Studies Department and in her various roles as Assistant Dean. Student classes, colleagues and audiences in attendance at her lectures, talks and poetry readings over the years have been mesmerized by her dynamic and riveting presentations.

Magic is the term that I would use to describe the chemistry between Sister Francesca and those fortunate to observe her. Sister Francesca has been a tremendous advocate for all students at Fordham, and she has been particularly effective in addressing the concerns of our students of color. She has spent many long days and nights on campus investigating and attempting to right possible injustices.

On a personal note, I have grown immeasurably through my own association with Sister Francesca. She has helped to renew and reaffirm my faith. The standards and expectations that she has set for students and professionals at Fordham have reaffirmed my own values. I have been delighted and proud to number Sister Francesca Thompson among my dearest friends and colleagues.

Sincerely,

Claude J. Mangum, Ph.D.
Associate Professor
African & African American Studies
Fordham University

*The "D-Men" Class of United Theological Seminary
(Class of 1999)
featuring two of our honorees, Rev. Dr. Otis Moss, Jr. and
Rev. Dr. Jeremiah A. Wright, Jr., along with their esteemed
professor, Rev. Dr. Samuel DeWitt Proctor*

PRINCETON
THEOLOGICAL SEMINARY

Rabbi, We know you are a teacher
who has come from God... John 3:2b

Samuel DeWitt Proctor Conference, Inc.
4533 South Lake Park Avenue
Chicago, Illinois 60653

I am pleased to write this letter for the fourth Samuel DeWitt Procter Conference honoring those who have made stellar contributions to the various dimensions of Christian witness in our nation. Thus, I can think of no one more deserving of such recognition than Professor James H. Cone, whose first book, ***Black Theology and Black Power,*** launched the Black Theology Movement nearly four decades ago. That work sent shock waves throughout the academic circles of theological and religious scholarship in this country and beyond. Who could have guessed that an angry young black man would find himself at the helm of a new, dynamic movement in theology destined to be a major catalyst for the gradual reshaping of theological education both nationally and globally.

Soon after Cone's book was published, The Society for the Study of Black Religion was formed. The late Dr. Shelby S. Rooks, Executive Director of the Fund for Theological Education, had already been deeply engaged in the task of reshaping African American ministry. His vision and organizational expertise played a major role in bringing the SSBR into existence. Then and now, that organization afforded the opportunity for the relatively few blacks in theological education to meet annually for the purpose of encouraging one another to weigh the implications of Cone's black theology not only for our various academic disciplines but also for the black churches.

Inspired by Cone's theology and the many criticisms and challenges of his colleagues, a new wave of black scholars was born. Their works soon expanded the breadth and depth of theological studies. Using the tools of many disciplines these scholars helped retrieve relevant resources in African American history and reconceptualize their meanings in light of the new insights provided by James Cone's challenging theology. Clearly, nothing would ever again be the same as it was prior to James Cone and for that we and generations yet to come will always be deeply indebted to him and his incredible genius.

With gratitude and best wishes always,

Peter J. Paris

Peter J. Paris, G. Homrighausen Professor of Christian Social Ethics

Princeton Theological Seminary • P.O. Box 821 • Princeton, NJ 08542-0803
Phone: 609.497.7814 • Fax: 609.497.7728 • Email: peter.paris@ptsem.edu

THE WORKS OF
Rev. Dr. James H. Cone

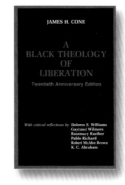

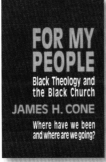

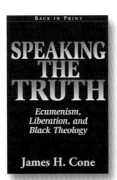

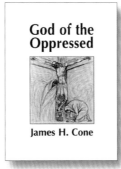

JUDGED FAITHFUL…..APPOINTED FOR SERVICE!

Dr. Thelma Davidson Adair

Reverend Euton E. Williams
Minister Member - Presbytery of New York City
Brooklyn, NY

Dr. Thelma Davidson Adair

Wife/Mother/Church Woman
Educator/Amicable/Community Activist/Compassionate

*I*have known Thelma D. Adair for more than fifty years. She is the proud mother of three children who have achieved marked excellence in their respective professions: physician, clergy and educator. They, of themselves, are the most tangible evidence of the impact her life has had on those who come under her influence.

I first met her and her late husband, Dr. Eugene A. Adair, in 1952, as a seminary intern from Union Theological Seminary. I remained associated with her work, ministry and career over these many years.

As a mother and student at Columbia University, she and her husband were pioneers in developing and housing day care programs in the church facilities for working parents of the community during the war years of the 1940s. That initiative later expanded into a community-wide "Early Childhood Education" program within the larger Harlem community consisting of: Head Start, day care, family day care and after school programs in tutoring, remediation and recreation.

Her interest in education placed her on the faculty of Queens College, City University of New York, a position she held for many years until her retirement in 1994. In 1996, she came out of retirement to head the education program she initiated as its executive director. She is a well-sought-after speaker in the areas of education, social witness, community and urban development.

Dr. Adair brings to all her work and endeavors a profound Christian faith, which serves as the foundation and motivating factor for her life and work.

Dr. Thelma D. Adair's life has been one of facing and conquering challenges and of creating pathways of opportunities for others. Her pathways are wide and inviting enough for others to venture forth and find acceptance, help, guidance and support.

LEGACY

Dr. Thelma Davidson Adair

"Ayekoo" - Divine Appreciation for The Sacrifice

Rev. Dr. Jeremiah A. Wright, Jr.

*I*first met Rev. Jeremiah Wright in Ghana during Trinity United Church of Christ's second homecoming tour of Ghana. I was the tour guide for the group that Dr. Wright led that year. He knew much more about Africa than I did, yet he paid attention to the commentaries I gave. Each morning, on these tours, he led the group in intense African oriented re-education. For the past nearly 10 years, I have consistently been the tour guide of Dr. Wright's groups to Ghana. I am almost always present because I gained lots of insight into our African heritage in these one hour morning interactions. I am more sensitive to African-American feelings and history, thanks to the re-orientation I receive at the feet of this great teacher. I am a better African Christian thanks to his sharing.

A couple of years ago, he took time off his often busy schedule and visited me in my home in a dusty little corner of Accra, Ghana's capital city. There, in the sweltering heat and humidity of Ghana's tropical weather, he met my wife and learned about my life history as school teacher, minister of Christ and tour professional. That he humbled himself and came down to my home in the "ghetto" in order to understand me makes me remember a similar example written for our edification in Philippians 2:3-11. In this crooked and self-centered world Rev. Wright shines bright like the stars in the universe. (Philippians 2:15).

Dr. Wright is a true African in his affections. The projects in several parts of Ghana that he and TUCC have initiated, executed and continue to support show that his heart is truly in Africa. His love for ordinary African people was shown in my life several years ago when he first sent me an invitation to visit the USA. When the visa application was first denied in 2001, I gave up. He did not. He persisted in his support, encouraged me to re-apply, and in 2005, I received the visa and became his guest at the Hampton University Ministers Conference. In 2006, I was again invited by Rev. Wright to the Samuel De Witt Proctor Conference in Florida. As the head of the Worldwide Church of God in Ghana, these sponsored invitations have been of immense benefit not only to me but to the 600 members and the leadership team of the church.

His selfless devotion to the welfare of others deserves my heartfelt ayekoo!!*

Beyond the concept of "thank you" to the divine meaning of "appreciation for the sacrifice."

Emmanuel Okai
Chairman, Ecclesiatical Council
Worldwide Church of God
Ghana, West Africa

HERITAGE AND HOPE FOR ALL SEASONS

Dr. Thelma Davidson Adair

Thelma C. Davidson Adair has witnessed and served from the overflow of her knowledge and experience for over a half century and counting. She continues to do so today through her message of heritage and hope that has been passed down to others who imbibed of her knowledge as she served as a mentor, friend, teacher, and confidante to them. Countless persons in the Presbyterian Church (U.S.A.), the ecumenical community, including Church Women United, Inc., the educational field, and the global community count her as friend, teacher, colleague, advocate, storyteller, and as partner in ministry. Her constellation of partners in ministry has been many; her constellation of gifts is manifold; her sharing of those gifts with partners in ministry continues ad infinitum.

She continues to be a "woman for all seasons." She has provided the creative seed, the catalyst, the prophetic challenge, the ardor and order for many activities in the faith community. Her signature has been one of a noble calling! I am, thus, pleased to add my signature to attest to how Thelma Adair's noble calling has led her to serve as a mentor and friend to many persons from the continent of Africa to the streets of New York City, to the city of Atlanta. This writer is one of the persons whom the witness and service of Thelma Adair touched in indelible ways.

God bless Dr. Thelma C. Davidson in these special days ahead.

Bettie J. Durrah
Elder/Lay Leader, Presbyterian Church (U.S.A.)

Rev. Dr. Jeremiah A. Wright, Jr.

To the Samuel DeWitt Proctor Committee:

I thank God that Rev. Dr. Jeremiah A. Wright, Jr. is blessed and highly favored! It is because of his favor with God that I have been blessed beyond measure.

I came to Trinity United Church of Christ in the early 1980's. When I arrived, I witnessed the equality of men and women, the inclusion of "whosoever will" and I heard the Word of God being preached and taught like I have never heard before. For the first time in my 22 years of being a follower of Christ, who I was as an African American, a woman and a Christian came to together, and I felt whole for the first time in my life.

After completing seminary I was privileged to serve for fourteen years under Pastor Wright's leadership. During those years I learned the importance of scholarship, knowing who we are as African people in Diaspora, and applying the Word of God to "this present age." I learned that the people cannot be free if they do not know where they have been, where they currently are and do not have a vision and plan for where they are going. Most importantly, I learned that Jesus was just as political as he was spiritual, and if, as ministers, we are not preaching and teaching the liberation ("setting the captives free") of the people of God, we are fleecing rather than feeding God's sheep.

Today I am the minister that I am because of Pastor Wright. I am the pastor of a new church start because of Pastor Wright. Grace United Church of Christ (Milwaukee, WI) is in existence because of Pastor Wright. The people in Milwaukee are being blessed because of Pastor Wright. The Wisconsin Conference is blessed because of Pastor Wright. Our entire denomination is blessed because of the preaching, teaching and ministry of Rev. Dr. Jeremiah A. Wright, Jr.

Rev. Wanda Washington
Grace United Church of Christ
Milwaukee, Wisconsin

Unsparing, Transparent and Faithful!

Rev. Dr. James H. Cone

For the last four decades, Dr. James H. Cone has been the preeminent voice of North American Black theological scholarship and consciousness. His initial writings on a Black theology of liberation were a shot across the bow of the academy and the church; countless books, articles and commentaries later, his thought continues to reverberate through our collective consciousness (***Malcolm & Martin & America*** has long been my favorite). Books and essays have been written in his honor and tenure and promotion gained as a consequence of his work. Activist-pastors have found wisdom in his pages and the Black faithful empowerment through his words.

> *...the critical distillation*
> *of mind and spirit,*
> *not one versus the other*
> *that so distinguishes the work*
> *of this seminal scholar.*

Dr. Cone's speech-acts are no less impactful. One need only recall Jim's poignant five minute address at Tavis Smiley's annual *State of the Black Union* in 2003 to know that his is a voice that rings powerfully and prophetically true. There is no ambiguity in his thinking where the liberation of peoples of African descent is concerned. Jim is that rare person of intellect who benefits from every theoretical and pragmatic progression crossing his threshold. From womanists, nationalists, global liberationists, eco-theologians, and more, he has learned. In short, he takes as well as he gives.

It is a truth: Jim does not suffer fools gladly when it comes to the rigorous engagement of the mind and the spirit. It is the critical distillation of mind and spirit, not one versus the other, that so distinguishes the work of this seminal scholar. He is unsparing in his critique, transparent in his person and faith to his calling. I am glad to call Jim Cone friend – and anticipate, with others, future outpourings of his mind and spirit. God is not through with him yet. May we long continue to be blessed by his searing witness.

Dr. Alton B. Pollard, III
Director of Black Church Studies
Associate Professor of Religion and Culture
Emory University - Candler School of Theology
Atlanta, GA

ST. ANTHONY MESSENGER PRESS

28 W. Liberty Street
Cincinnati, OH 45202-6498
PHONE 513-241-5615
FAX 513-241-0399
E-MAIL StAnthony@
AmericanCatholic.org

NATIONAL CATHOLIC MAGAZINE

St. Anthony Messenger

BOOKS

St. Anthony Messenger Press
Servant Books

FAITH FORMATION RESOURCES

Catholic Update
Every Day Catholic
Bringing Home the Word
Homily Helps
Weekday Homily Helps

ELECTRONIC MEDIA

Audiobooks

Video
Catholic Update Video
Franciscan Communications

Internet
AmericanCatholic.org
FranciscanRadio.org

Sr. Francesca Thompson, OSF

October 9, 2006

Samuel DeWitt Proctor Conference
4353 Lake Park Avenue
Chicago, IL 60653

Dear Friends,

It was my priviledge to pester Franciscan Sister Francesca Thompson at great length on several occasions so I could craft a modest article for our national Catholic magazine, **St. Anthony Messenger** (February 2006). I say "modest" because my mandate was to profile this great woman in 2500 words! I take this opportunity to apologize for all that was left out.

I did not confess there that I have known Francesca for more than 40 years and have found her gracious, tolerant and consistently able to serve as a bridge, translator, consummate communicator and evangelist for education and equality. She is as devoted a follower of St. Francis of Assisi as any Franciscan I know.

While her feet have walked with giants, she has never tried to lead the parade.

While her feet have walked on the path of St. Francis, she has invited people of all faiths and none to walk with her.

While her feet are black and beautiful, she has walked nobly with people of all colors and races, endeavoring to enlarge the path of diversity and acceptance toward a Promised Land of equal opportunity.

While her feet have carried her abroad, she cherishes her Indiana roots and is a prophet in her own land. As a fellow Hoosier, I take heart in that--and in all that Francesca has spoken with an eloquence that beats down prejudice and lifts up culture and candor.

Sincerely,

Carol Ann Morrow
Assistant Editor

PROPHETIC SEER

Rev. Dr. James H. Cone

Honor is something people like James Cone do not seek, and it is hard for them to imagine why it is necessary particularly when justice is waiting to be born in the reality of people of color around the globe. For over forty years, James Cone has unceasingly been committed to black liberation theology as his Christian passion for truth and justice. Without the display of his Christian and intellectual passion for truth, courage and pioneering theological vision for justice, the voice of black churches, the people who frequent its pews and the story of those who suffer oppression would not be heard.

Any tribute to James Cone must see his theological work and scholarly labors as a devotion to the faith tradition of the black church that produced and gifted him with the insight of a prophetic seer who refuses to compromise Jesus' liberating message for our day and time. James Cone has demonstrated both in the theological academy and in the church that "the God of the Oppressed" is truly his God, and is the God with whom we must deal and whose "will" must guide our decisions and actions.

...with the insight of a prophetic seer who refuses to compromise Jesus' liberating message for our day and time

Forrest E. Harris
Director, Kelly Miller Smith Institute on Black Church Studies
Vanderbilt University Divinity School

President, American Baptist College
Nashville, Tennessee

VOICE IN A DRY LAND –
FOOTPRINTS OF A PROPHET

Rev. Dr. Jeremiah A. Wright, Jr.

It is both appropriate, necessary and long overdue that we celebrate and honor the life and ministry of Rev. Jeremiah A. Wright, Jr. I will be forever grateful personally for his friendship and mentoring in my life, and for being one whom I can share my faith, struggles and dreams with. But Jeremiah Wright is a gift and treasure to the body of Christ and one who I know has given creditability to this institution called church that Jesus left us, and one whom I know the Father has been able to look down on over and over throughout his ministry and say, this is My son in whom I am well pleased!

Rev. Wright has been a prophetic voice in a dry land; he has laid out for us a blueprint for ministry with integrity and he has been true to the liberation message of the Gospel of Jesus Christ in a time when the church seems to be committed to helping people adjust to Pharaoh, rather than be freed!

Rev. Wright has spent his life confronting the unequal playing fields of our society, teaching both from the pulpit and from his personal witness that faith is not just to help us endure, but it is also the weapon with which we must fight to win and until we win.

Rev. Wright's foundation has always been his faith and his deep love for God. It is no question that Jesus is indeed his first love and that he has placed his life firmly in His hand. This has been his strength and his power.

Rev. Wright has not only given us a model for pastoring, but he has shown us you can still be a loving, dedicated and present father and husband. His love for his children and for his wonderful wife Ramah is real, lived and consistent.

Rev. Wright has also presented a standard for ministry that demanded excellence and expected training and preparation, along with calling and anointing. He has made it clear after one is called by God, the people of God deserve a minister who has had the educational preparation and formation to best serve them.

Rev. Wright has also shown us that one does not have to leave their faith to find the affirmation of one's Blackness and to be true to one's culture and race. He has unashamedly spoken truth to power and found his power in truth! He has laid down his life for his God, for the people he was called to pastor and for all of us who have been formed, shaped and touched by his witness, faith and sacrificial love!

This has not been without cost! This prophetic witness has cost him both criticism and attack, both from the pews in his church and the countless voices outside that have sought to attack him usually from jealousy and envy and sometimes because it exposed their own weak ministry of compromise and sell out!

Thank you Jeremiah for refusing to bow to man! Thank you for refusing to drink from the cup of compromise. Thank you for speaking the truth in season and out of season! Thank you for being true to your God. Thank you for enduring the pain and for leading even where it was lonely. Thank you for modeling authentic ministry. Thank you for consistently opening the rivers of righteousness and the streams of Justice. Thank you for your unwavering faith, unconditional love and unending sense of humor and laughter amidst it all!

Finally, thank you for being my hero and my brother!

Rev. Dr. Michael L. Pfleger, Pastor
The Faith Community of Saint Sabina

DR. THELMA DAVIDSON ADAIR A.K.A. LADY ADIAR

Dr. Thelma Davidson Adair

With the rapid pace of our modern world where life without some form of technology is unthinkable and where the focus is on consumerism and competition, are octogenarians still relevant? Do they understand the current realities and sensibilities of today's children, young adults and even their baby boomer offspring?

For three decades I have had the opportunity of knowing and interacting with a woman who has traversed eight decades and at each one left an indelible impression upon those who had the privilege of meeting her. Even as a young girl, it is my understanding, that the brilliant sparkle in her eyes, the radiance of her smile and her insatiable appetite for learning singled her as a child of promise; a child who would forge ahead conquering new frontiers and contributing to humanity with the goal being to make the world a better place for all mankind, irrespective of racial, gender type or economic background. As herstory goes, she very early on became a crusader for economic, gender and racial equality and did not resign herself to the rhetoric of the hour but instead put the rubber to the road learning and allowing her inquisitive mind to concoct ideas taking her into unchartered places in the world, which later she would visit. Age has not dulled her mind, and if anything, she is more incisive today than perhaps twenty years ago. Her aptitude of local, national and international issues is amazing. She is imbued with a moral compass that continues to compel her to be a vocal spokeswoman on matters of racial, gender, class and social injustices for all sectors of society.

The woman to whom I make reference is known to flip the script in pursuit of justice and equality. She is a woman of undeniable integrity and relentless courage and insight. Her personal and professional accomplishments are secondary to her quest to be the caliber of person who leads by example. The woman whom I am writing about is uniquely special for her mantra is to create access to opportunities, to nurture success and to foster transformation.

So are octogenarians relevant in the 21st century, where the focus is on Prada, expensive technological devices and Ludacris? Dr. Thelma Davidson Adair is far more relevant today than she was 60 years ago when she, her late husband, Rev. Eugene Adair, and their eldest son arrived in New York City from Chester, South Carolina. Lady Adair, a sobriquet given to her years ago, is a traveler who has dined with royalty on several continents but always seeks the comforts of home, family and friends in the Harlem community where she is respected, held in high esteem and has resided for more than sixty years. Thelma Davidson Adair's enthusiasm for life and the living arouses much interest from younger people who are awestruck by her physical stamina and mental acumen. Lady Adair has the uncanny ability to mesmerize audiences of all ages with her experiences from near and afar and adeptly makes a connection so they can understand the significance of being citizens of the world.

Dr. Thelma Davidson Adair is one of the saints in my life for whom I have enormous respect and love. There are two words which truly describe this extraordinary woman: phenomenal octogenarian.

Dr. Kenneth C. Boatner

Rev. Dr. Jeremiah A. Wright, Jr.

Tribute to My Senior Pastor

Unashamedly Black and Unapologetically Christian, when I saw this motto in print in 1979, I was excited and challenged.

When I heard and later met the man who had been entrusted to build a ministry using this phrase, Rev. Dr. Jeremiah A. Wright, Jr., my excitement increased and the challenge became greater.

Now, 28 years, later after journeying with my Senior Pastor and gaining an even greater understanding of these words, I can proclaim that both the excitement and challenge are at their zenith.

My ministry started with the Baptist General Conference of America, a Swedish Baptist denomination. We were of fundamental and evangelical. We believed in formal training and correct study. A clear understanding of doctrine and the ability to express that doctrine were critical.

I knew that my training had been excellent… then I met Rev. Jeremiah A. Wright Jr. I soon realized that there was a need for more work on my part.

In the early days at 400 W. 95th, my greatest learning occurred before the worship services. We would sit in his office and he began to teach me what I now call "The Blackenization of my Theology." He not only "Blackenized" my theology, my teaching, my preaching and my ministry, but in so doing, I was Set Free to Be!!

His brilliance, his eloquence, his scholarship, his penmanship are known throughout the World.

I am blessed, that he allows me to call him my "Baby Brother" and, more importantly, "My Friend."

Rev. Dr. Clyde A. White

Rev. Dr. Otis Moss Jr.

ANDREW YOUNG

*I*n any list of superlatives pertaining to preachers, pastors, prophets, scholars, and saints of our time, Otis Moss, Jr. will emerge on the top in any category. If you're talking of persons of exemplary talents who also excel in spiritual gifts, he almost stands alone.

Of course, I say this as a friend and brother, which is even more remarkable when you think of it.

In this world of competitive egos and images, Dr. Moss emerges as everyone's friend and confidant. More so, important people turn to him for guidance and counsel than almost any spiritual leader I know.

Dr. Moss reflects the character of his mentors: Benjamin Mays and Martin Luther King, Jr. in his university, political and community service.

Dr. Moss does not need or want a tribute but we do ourselves a great disservice when we don't fully appreciate true greatness walking among us.

Congratulations and Best Wishes.

Peace and Blessings,

Ambassador Andrew Young
Chairman, GoodWorks International

"Blessed is the servant who keeps the secret of the Lord in [her] heart."

St. Francis of Assisi

Sr. Francesca Thompson, OSF

**Teacher, Poet, Administrator, Gifted Writer, Lecturer, Director,
Cherished Relative and Friend, Giver of Self, Faithful Servant of the Lord.**

These are all words that might be used to describe Sister Francesca Thompson, OSF. Without a doubt, Sister Francesca is a most talented and dedicated person. She has used her talents well in the field of education. But the one attribute that stands out in Francesca's life is her unqualified dedication to the service of the Lord. As a Franciscan Sister, she has allowed the spirit of St. Francis to come alive in her and in doing so has been a catalyst for change in every venue in which she has found herself. Although Francesca has never been shy in expressing herself, her thoughts are always delivered with forethought and grace, concern for the feelings of others, a great deal of compassion and often with a touch of humor. Francesca has delivered the Gospel message of love to all with whom she has come in contact. Her joy in living the Gospel lights up a room when she walks in and her warm smile says that she accepts all as her brothers and sisters.

We, as members of your religious community, congratulate you on being an honoree this evening. We applaud you and we wish you well. We are proud to call you our sister and fellow traveler on the Gospel journey. You have let your life speak, and in doing so, you have followed the admonition of Francis to preach the Gospel in all places and if need be to use words. Congratulations and we love you.

Sister Rose Lima

AN AMAZING WONDER

Rev. Dr. Jeremiah A. Wright, Jr.

*"For it is God who is at work within you, giving you the will
and power to achieve His purpose."*
Phil 2:13

Dear Rev. Wright,

The manifestation of the will of God in your life is apparent to all with eyes to see and ears to hear. In 1979, when Iva, my daughter, joined Trinity United Church of Christ after a four generation family membership of 66 years in the same church, I just knew she had "hooked up" with a cult. I went "bananas." I wanted to consign the preacher, whomever he was, to the lowest region of HELL.

Ten years later, Mama followed child and planted her feet on solid and fertile ground. As I look back over the past, I realize people come into your life for a reason, a season, or a life time. In God's time you, Rev. Wright, entered my life. And now I can proclaim, "I wouldn't take nothing for my journey. What a blessing!"

I am honored and elated to witness and share in this occasion of celebrating you, your mission and your ministry. I write out of deep respect and love for you whom I have come to know in a very special way.

God granted you many gifts and experiences. You have not squandered any of them – from medicine to music; from humor to the holy; from recitation to application; from preacher to prophet; from foreign languages to ebonics. All roads lead to a preacher/prophet and pastor/shepherd who knows and feeds his sheep throughout the world - giving the sheep the food they need, not necessarily what they want. To worship, study and travel with you in Africa, Brazil and throughout this nation have challenged me and others to experience the profound difference between belonging to a church and being the church.

You are consistently constant, candid, compassionate, courageous, determined and relevant. One needs not speculate about your opinion, will or whom you serve. You are an open book whose genius is imbued with humility and integrity. Excellence is your trademark.

Our relationship as pastor to parishioner, teacher to learner, friend to friend and yes, even mother to son is, I know, a gift from God. As we continue to share deep valley and mountain top experiences, the bonds of our journey are sealed by an unconditional faith to a God we serve.

God's gift to the world, through the handiworks and footprints of your ministry, is as eternal as those of the biblical prophet Jeremiah. The legacy of your life's achievements will build bridges for generations yet to come.

In the words of your Aunt Hattie, you are indeed "an amazing wonder." I know Mama and Daddy Wright continue to say, "This is Jeremiah, my beloved son in whom I am well pleased." You are my theological son, for whom I am truly grateful. Each and every day, I thank God for your presence in my life. I pray that through it all, you remain encouraged and strengthened by His will, peace, power, mercy and grace.

Momma Lois
Lois B. Johnson

A TRIBUTE TO DADDY

Rev. Dr. Jeremiah A. Wright, Jr.

From the days of playing "Lick 'n Stick" (the game, named after one of James Brown's greatest hits of the '60s), while running free in the yard of our apartment complex in Seat Pleasant, Maryland, to date, Daddy has been our hero. As we spent time praying and preparing to write this tribute to the most phenomenal man in our lifetime, Janet and I began to share thoughts and stories of childhood in the 1960s through present day.

As we look back over the years, remembering Daddy as the driver for our nursery school (pre-Chicago days), we paused to thank God for the blessing of the experience. The experience is one unmatched and unequal to any other experience of our lifetime. The experience is one that not only drove us back and forth to nursery school in a VW Volkswagen station wagon, but the experience is one that made sure our lives began on an even keel, as he held us and rocked us to sleep every night as babies.

When we think about Daddy, our **first** thoughts are "Dog Team! 'Woof'" Being put to bed at night by Daddy and us wanting to be Que Dogs for as long as we can remember! Stepping to bed as little Omega Pearls with Daddy leading his little pack!

Experiencing Daddy ~

Always knowing the songs to every hot R&B song (and making sure that we knew the words too), as well as taking us to church every Sunday…Taking us on road trips to Philadelphia, DC/Maryland and "Six Flags."

…Traveling with him as he preached his trial sermons at all those churches, until we knew the entire sermon and would preach it with him… Watching him have faith in God and telling us that the little church on 95th Street was where God was placing him, and that one day Trinity was going to be a great church, and was an awesome opportunity for growth in ministry.

…Making us sing duets in church! "Through It All!"

…Learning that Daddy is a man first --- a man touched by God --- and a pastor to so many people! Going to visit the sick and watching Daddy minister to people; going to lectures and workshops with him, and sitting in awe as Daddy spoke from the top of his head; going to Greater Harvest Baptist Church on Sunday nights, and eating Lem's barbecue after the radio broadcast service.

The experience exposed (and still continues to expose) us to all people from all walks of life, watching, and learning how to interact with any and everyone because we are all children of God!

We could go on and on, but due to space limitations, we can only share a fraction of the experience of Daddy. We know that we are truly blessed to have been born to this Man of God, son of Jeremiah and Mary, "Buddy," Jerry "Que Dog," Rev., our Daddy! How do we say thanks for the things that he has done for us?!!!! To God be the glory!

Janet & Jeri

FAMILY MAN

Rev. Dr. Jeremiah A. Wright, Jr.

Your presence in our lives has taught us what the true meaning of FAMILY is. You are the epitome of a family man: Exuding love, togetherness, extending yourself and doing all you can to adjust your extraordinarily busy schedule so we can just be with you and with each other. Whether in the house, in the church, or on vacation, you are and continue to be a living example of a true family man!

Giving tirelessly of yourself to all of God's people, while living through family problems, family trouble, family drama, continues to amaze us and confirm for each of us that you are the man God has called you to be. We thank God that you have been able to deal with family stuff in the midst of all the church mess (oops!), church growth, and not lost your mind, shot anybody, or sent anyone to prison or to their grave. We thank God that you let nothing get in the way of being present in our lives!

We thank God for the man we know, and few others experience! We thank God for the laughter, the tears, the jokes, the antagonizing, the spirit of Mary and Jeremiah that oozes out of you in all you do, and for the countless lessons you teach us in your every day living! Words will never suffice the debt of gratitude we owe you. We are because you are!

Lovingly,

Your Family

Rev. Dr. Jeremiah A. Wright, Jr.

Sr. Francesca Thompson, OSF

Dr. Thelma Davidson Adair

Rev. Dr. Otis Moss, Jr.

Rev. Dr. Jeremiah A. Wright, Jr.

Rev. Dr. James H. Cone

QUOTES FROM HONOREES

"...we have the responsibilities to develop creative theology that will hold us accountable to the gospel of Jesus Christ…We need to nurture a critical and prophetic theology to effectively minister to our congregations. We can develop great rhetorical skills, create effective programs of stewardship, discover ingenious schemes for church growth and management, and find creative ways to mobilize and fight for justice in society. But if we don't have a clear understanding of what the gospel means, we are lost and all the other things we do are meaningless."

Rev. Dr. James H. Cone

"… at the top and bottom of Jesus' text is theology, and in between it's economics, politics and sociology. Therefore if you are preaching a gospel that has nothing about politics…economics…sociology, you are preaching an empty gospel…It might be a popular gospel, but it's not powerful. It might be expedient and safe, but it's not saving. We need prophets in this age in which prophets are not liked."

Rev. Dr. Otis Moss, Jr.

"No man ever took his hat out of the ring when other men ran against him. I decided if we were going to run, we had to be competitive and play by the rules…There is a need for women to encourage and support other women in leadership roles. In some ways we are not as assertive as I would hope for us to be."

Dr. Thelma Adair

"Martin Luther King's powerful message at Riverside launched a frontal attack against a government which had us in an immoral, illegal, unwinnable and based-on-a-presidential-lie war in Vietnam. We are only able to enjoy the quality of life that we have in the USA by keeping people in the developing countries…making less than two dollars a day. King came out on the side of the poor….We couldn't hear King then. My question remains, "Can you hear him now?""

Rev. Dr. Jeremiah A. Wright, Jr.

"I believe that who we are says more than what we say we are."

Sister Francesca

A CALL TO RENEWAL! 2007!

ACKNOWLEDGEMENTS

The Baobab tree symbolizes the spirit of our reverence for those we honor. It is considered to be a sacred tree of knowledge and life. It is alternatively known as "Mother" by African people. Often mistaken for dead, this fascinating tree, whose life spans have been recorded from 1000-4000 years, is much alive and full of resources. Peoples come to the Baobab tree to pray, to gather honey, to pick fruit, and to find medicinal herbs. The tree nourishes many small and large animals of the savannah. Even in times of drought, the Baobab tree has proven to be a source of water. The African proverb says, "Wisdom is like a Baobab tree, no one person can embrace it." And so it is with those we honor in this volume: their life and gifts of ministry will nourish many for generations yet to come.

The eternal gifts of the Spirit are manifested through the lives and life achievements of those we celebrate in the fourth volume of *Beautiful Are Their Feet*. This volume chronicles only a glimpse of the legacy of these prophets. May our children and our children's children know of their good works. May our footprints be found on the paths that they have so sacrificially created.

I am truly grateful to Dr. Maurice McNeil for shepherding the process that brought this volume to fruition. I thank all those who gave of their time and talents to bring to life this fourth volume of *Beautiful Are Their Feet*.

Dr. Iva E. Carruthers
2007

Herbert Allen
Rev. Joan Harrell
Rev. Thelma Hogg
Ms. Lois Johnson
Dr. Maurice McNeil
L. Julie Torrey Parker
Katara Washington